D0060138

LOS GATOS PUBLIC LIBRARY

A Fistful of Rice

A Fistful of Rice

of Rice

My Unexpected Quest to End

Poverty Through Profitability

VIKRAM AKULA

LOS GATOS PUBLIC LIBRARY
LOS GATOS, CALIFORNIA

HARVARD BUSINESS REVIEW PRESS

BOSTON, MASSACHUSETTS

Copyright 2011 Vikram Akula

All rights reserved

Printed in the United States of America

14 13 12 11 10   5 4 3 2 1

No part of this publication may be reproduced, stored in, or introduced into
a retrieval system, or transmitted, in any form or by any means (electronic,
mechanical, photocopying, recording, or otherwise), without the prior
permission of the publisher. Requests for permission should be directed to
permissions@hbsp.harvard.edu, or mailed to Permissions, Harvard Business
School Publishing, 60 Harvard Way, Boston, Massachusetts 02163.

Library of Congress Cataloging-in-Publication Data

Akula, Vikram.
   A fistful of rice : my unexpected quest to end poverty through
   profitability / Vikram Akula.
      p. cm.
   ISBN 978-1-4221-3117-6 (hbk. : alk. paper)   1. Akula, Vikram.
   2. Microfinance—India.   3. Poverty—India.   I. Title.
   HG178.33.I4A48 2010
   332—dc22
   [B]   2011030663

The paper used in this publication meets the requirements of the American
National Standard for Permanence of Paper for Publications and Documents
in Libraries and Archives Z39.48-1992.

This book is dedicated to my parents,

Akula V. Krishna and Padma Krishna.

I am grateful for your love and support.

CONTENTS

CHAPTER ONE

"Am I Not Poor, Too?"

IT WAS THE SUMMER of 1995 when a woman in rural India asked the simple, five-word question that changed my life.

I was an idealistic graduate student, working in India on a Fulbright scholarship and determined to change the world. This was my second stint working in remote Indian villages with the nonprofit Deccan Development Society (DDS), but my first time working in microfinance. The possibilities of microfinance—lending very small amounts of money to very poor people—seemed limitless, and I was excited to be learning about it on the ground.

As head of an agricultural lending program serving thirty villages, I'd putter down dirt roads on an Indian-made Hero Honda motorbike, meeting with borrowers, disbursing loans, and collecting repayments. Each week, I talked with rural Indians who were pulling themselves out of poverty and despair—landless laborers who had started with nothing but were now launching their own small businesses, earning not only money but greater self-respect as well.

The degree of poverty in these remote Indian villages was unlike anything I'd ever seen in the United States. Children with spindly legs and hungry eyes played in the mud alongside mangy stray dogs and farm animals. Piles of garbage dotted village roadsides, and sewage ran in trenches alongside homes. People lived in one-room mud huts, sweltering in the Indian sun. There was a smell of desperation in the air, a sense of resignation that went back centuries. The poor had always been poor, and here in the Indian hinterlands, it felt like they always would be.

Working to help these villagers was incredibly gratifying, though there were definitely hardships to living in remote villages: sleeping on a straw mat on the floor in a small room, fetching drinking water from a distant well, and seeing the effects of poor nutrition and hygienic conditions all around me was certainly a far cry from the middle-class comfort of Schenectady, New York, where I had grown up. But I felt like I was really making a difference, really helping to end poverty in India.

Then, one day, a woman walked into our regional office. Barefoot, emaciated, and wearing a faded purple sari, she was obviously poor and from a lower caste. But she'd found her way to our office because she'd heard about our program and wanted to learn more. This was no small achievement, as she'd either paid to take a bus or had walked quite a distance to find us.

She asked some questions about our lending, then got quickly to her point. "Can you start this program in my village?" she asked.

I looked closely at her. She was probably in her mid-thirties, but like many poor Indians, she looked older than her years. Her face was worn and her skin weathered, but her eyes were alight with purpose. Life had beaten her down, but it hadn't beaten the hope out of her. This, I thought, was exactly the kind of person we should be lending to. So I promised to ask DDS's director later that day.

Yet when I asked him if we could start lending in the woman's village, I got a disappointing answer. "Our grant cycle is coming to an end, Vikram," he told me. "We don't have the funds to expand right now beyond the villages we're already in. There's nothing we can do."

The next day, I rode my motorbike to the woman's village to break the news to her. The sudden appearance of an

Indian man speaking Telugu, the local language, with an American accent always caused a stir in remote villages, and it didn't take long for word to spread. The woman soon came outside to meet me.

"Here's the situation," I told her. "We don't have the resources right now to expand to new villages. We've got a set amount of money, and we've already committed it elsewhere." Even as the words came out of my mouth, I wished I could take them back. But all I could say was, "I'm very sorry."

The woman looked me in the eye, and with great dignity, she spoke the words that would change my life. "Am I not poor, too?" she asked me. I stared at her, jarred by the question, and she went on. "Do I not deserve a chance to get my family out of poverty?"

Am I not poor, too? With these words, this driven, determined woman suddenly made me see how unfair—unjust, really—our microfinance program was. Yes, we were helping hundreds of poor Indians take the first steps to pull themselves out of poverty. But my program had just $250,000 to spend in thirty villages—that was all DDS had been given for the project. And once that money was disbursed, there was no money left for other poor Indians who desperately wanted a chance too.

This woman wasn't asking for a dole. She wasn't asking for a handout. She was simply asking for an opportunity. But we couldn't give it to her.

This was a defining moment for me. We had to find a way to change microfinance—to make it available to any Indian, or any poor person anywhere in the world for that matter, who wanted to escape poverty. Microfinance was a fantastic tool, but a deeply flawed one. There simply had to be a way to scale it beyond the constraints of how it was currently being practiced.

I rode my motorbike home over those same dirt roads, but everything had changed. I had a new mission: to solve the problem of how to make microloans available on a mass scale, far larger than the few million people worldwide who were then being served. The search for that solution—and the incredible results, white-hot controversy, and vigorous ongoing debate it engendered—is what this book is about.

Like many people, I believe microfinance is a core solution to the global poverty problem. It provides poor people with the tools to find their own way out of poverty. It puts the power squarely in their hands, giving them a larger stake in their own success than simple one-time donations of food, goods, or cash. And it offers innumerable side benefits—not only to the poor themselves, but to economies, banking systems, and political systems where microfinance is practiced. It is an incredibly powerful, versatile tool.

But unlike some, I believe that microfinance institutions, or MFIs, must be set up as highly commercial, for-profit entities if we have any hope of eradicating poverty.

This point of view puts me at odds with many of my colleagues, but it's one I feel very strongly about. So strongly, in fact, that in late 1997 I started my own company, SKS Microfinance, to do just that. We launched as a nonprofit out of necessity, but the goal was always to turn it into a for-profit company, which we did in 2005.

Many of the people I've worked with over the years—people whose opinions I respect, and whose love for India and desire to help the poor are deeply felt—have expressed keen disappointment in my choice. They say it's unacceptable, even unethical, to make money from charging interest on loans to the poor. But I believe the opposite: that doing well by doing good is not only acceptable, it's absolutely ethical. In fact, I believe that offering microfinance as a highly commercial, for-profit venture is the *more* ethical choice, by far.

I didn't come to these beliefs overnight. They're the culmination of a journey, one that took me through the worlds of academia, philosophy, nonprofits, and business. But the very first step of that journey was discovering what poverty really was, as a young boy visiting India.

THOUGH I WAS BORN in the south Indian city of Hyderabad, my family immigrated to the United States in 1970, as part of the "brain drain" that led so many educated Indians to seek their fortunes abroad. My father, Akula

Krishna, a surgeon, brought us to upstate New York when I was two to start our new lives. Years later, when I went back as an adult to live in poverty-stricken rural India, my parents were baffled: why would I return to such a place, after they'd taken such pains to create a better, more comfortable life for us in America?

The answer lay in a few grains of rice. When I was about seven, my parents took me back to India for the first time to visit with family. I had no memory of my first two years there, and thought of myself as fully American. But during that trip, India made an impression on me that I would never forget.

I was at my aunt's house, a comfortable home in a middle-class Hyderabad neighborhood, when someone knocked at her door. It was a woman with a half-dozen steel pots and a young boy in tow. She was selling the pots door to door. And by the look of her sari and her drawn, sallow face, she desperately needed whatever she could get in barter for them.

My aunt invited the woman in and began looking over her wares, while her son hovered near the doorway, unsure whether he was allowed to come in. As children do, he and I shyly sized each other up. It was clear from his dirty clothes and gaunt frame that he and I lived in completely different worlds, but he was about my age, so I felt a kind of connection with him right away. We didn't speak, but we continued to eye each other as my aunt and his mother bartered over what she would receive in exchange for the pots.

A price was agreed upon, and my aunt went into the kitchen to bring out rice for payment. I watched as the woman squatted down and held out her *pallu*, the folds of her sari. My aunt poured the rice grains into the out-stretched garment, and a few grains—maybe fifteen in all—fell to the floor. The floor was made of dark, shiny *shabbad* stones, so the smattering of white grains stood out. I figured my aunt would just sweep them away when the woman and her son left.

To my astonishment, the woman reached down and pressed her finger against each grain to pick it up. My aunt was already heading back to the kitchen with her rice con-tainer, but this woman was carefully scouring the floor, making sure she hadn't missed a single grain. This, I sud-denly realized, was what it meant to be truly hungry.

Like most middle-class American kids, I'd heard the re-frain, "Don't waste your food! There are children starving in India." I was a conscientious child, so I always did try to eat everything I was served. But watching this boy and his mother, I understood for the first time that hunger was not an abstraction. These were real people—people not so dif-ferent from myself—and fifteen grains of rice really mat-tered for them.

If I had grown up in India, I doubt I'd have been struck at all by the scene that unfolded in my aunt's house that day. But I was an Indian boy growing up American in Schenectady, New York. I went to Cub Scouts, to birthday parties, to restaurants with my family. We lacked nothing, and we also weren't confronted with the daily reality of others' poverty: I was growing up in a happy, insulated bubble. But in India, poverty and hunger were right there for all to see—even right in my aunt's house. The contrast was stark and unforgettable.

We continued to go to Hyderabad over the summers, when I was out of school. I practiced my rudimentary Telugu, and kept learning more about India each time we visited. But I still considered myself 100 percent American, and even had asked my friends to call me Vic, rather than Vikram, so I could fit in better as I moved up through junior high school. Then, the summer I was twelve, I witnessed another incident in India that struck me as powerfully as the rice grains incident had five years earlier.

We had gone back for a family wedding, which in India, as in many parts of the developing world, is quite a lavish affair even if you're solidly middle class. Families will save money for years in order to put on the most extravagant celebration possible, with multiple courses served at the meal, fancy decorations, expensive gifts, and even rented camels or elephants for the bride and groom to ride in on.

Everyone was dressed in beautiful silk saris and ornate *kurtas*, with the women's gold jewelry glinting in the evening light. When we sat down for dinner, waiters brought out the food on traditional leaf plates. Course after course was served—piping-hot chicken biryani, glistening ghee-laden curries, sweet meat, dal, paneer, and sugary jelabi—with the waiters swiftly refilling each half-empty plate, as everyone ate and drank and the volume of the party increased.

Finally, the last course was finished. The happy, sated guests rose to begin migrating from the dining tent to another tent for the continued celebration. As I walked away from my table, I happened to glance back as the last leaf plates were being cleared.

Two boys about my age, in threadbare clothes and with lean, hungry faces, had made their way into the open-air dining tent. I watched as they took as many leaf plates as they could and carried them a short distance away, to the top of a hillock. They sat beneath a tree there, then quickly got to work: one boy scraped the leftover food off plates while the second, older boy held another plate to collect it all. Then the two boys, clearly ravenous, began scooping the leftovers into their mouths.

I stood and stared. I couldn't believe their desperation, literally eating our castoffs, our waste. In Schenectady, I thought, these boys might be my friends, or on my soccer team. Here, they were scavengers, too hungry to care who might see them filching the scraps of food we didn't want. It felt so unreal to me—and yet I was standing here, watching it happen. I almost couldn't stand that such desperation existed, and that it was on view, right there in front of me.

That was the moment I knew, beyond doubt, what I would do when I got older: I wanted to come back to India and help people like those boys get out of poverty. Why should I have an easy, comfortable life while others, by luck of the draw, had to struggle so hard to survive? It's probably too clear-cut, or too romanticized to say I made a vow right then to try and eliminate poverty in India. But that was the moment when what I'd seen lodged so firmly in my consciousness that I couldn't imagine doing anything else.

INDIA IS A LAND of breathtaking beauty, deep history, and astonishing diversity. It's a land with so many languages and dialects that fewer than half its people claim the national language, Hindi, as their native tongue. Depending on which city or village you go to, you're as likely to hear Bengali, Telugu, Urdu, Malayam, Punjabi—or English—as you are Hindi. All told, the country has fifteen official languages and hundreds of distinct dialects.

It is also a land of amazing religious and ethnic diversity. Though more than 80 percent of Indians identify as Hindu, a walk down any street in any city will take you past Muslim mosques, Sikh temples, Zoroastrian shrines, and Christian churches. And even within the Hindu religion, a plethora of gods vies for attention: Shiva, Ganesh, Krishna, Rama, and literally hundreds of others. Hindu temples, from sprawling complexes to tiny roadside shrines, pay homage to a vast and vibrant religious culture.

To be Indian is to share in a heritage that's at once common to a billion others and unique to each family, region, or faith. India is impossible to characterize in a few words; it is as colorful and chaotic as the wild, lurching traffic that flows through its streets. It is full of the hope and potential of an emerging economic power, and the excitement of becoming a potent new force in the world. And with its call centers, software developers, and eager embrace of the technology age, it is poised to enter a new era.

Yet India is also a land of extreme poverty. According to figures released by the World Bank in December of 2008, based on the results of the 2005 International Comparison Program (ICP), fully 42 percent of India's people live in poverty—meaning they exist on the purchase-power equivalent of less than $1.25 per day. With a population of more than 1 billion, that works out to more than 450 million poor people—more than the populations of the United States, Germany, and France put together.

If that's not bad enough, the numbers spike even more when you consider how many Indians live below the level of just $2 per day. According to the same World Bank report, 828 million Indians live at this standard—a number that represents more than 12 percent of the Earth's people, or greater than the populations of the United States, Russia, Germany, France, the United Kingdom, Italy, Spain, and Canada combined.

This is a stunning statistic, and not only in terms of pure numbers. Here's one more figure to put it into perspective: quoting again from the World Bank, those 828 million Indians living on less than $2 a day make up 75.6 percent of India's population. By comparison, in sub-Saharan Africa, generally considered the most poverty-stricken region in the world, 72.2 percent of the population lives at or below that standard. In India, poverty is a part of the landscape, as natural and unchanging as the vast Deccan plains and the flow of the Ganges River.

It's not simply that you notice the poverty when you visit India. It is all around you, so prevalent and insistent that you can see it, smell it, feel it, taste it. From the dusty villages scattered over bone-dry plains to the crumbling slums of the cities, the culture of poverty is embedded in the land. Anyone who's spent time in India returns home with stories of beggars lining the streets and mothers with hungry children in their laps, hands held out for a coin or two.

When I enrolled at Tufts University at seventeen, I began thinking in earnest about how to help India's poor. I devoured the works of the great philosophers, searching for clues on how to live my life and make a difference in the lives of others. Like many college students, I was drawn to leftist ideals, but I also craved the order and drive associated with the right. During my freshman year, in a moment of teenage zeal, I wrote in my journal that I wanted to "eradicate poverty with the discipline of a Marine." It was a strange, and rather corny, thing to write. But I was anxious not simply to *do* something, but to do it well and efficiently.

I became the do-gooder to end all do-gooders, spending my time studying, playing for the college tennis team, and working with the campus community service organization. While others went out on Friday nights, I volunteered at a local homeless shelter, as if trying to make up for the fact that I had so much while others had so little. I was driven by guilt, buried under the weight of my good fortune and the memory of the poverty I'd seen. And my fertile, overheated conscience was further pricked by reading Nietzsche my freshman year: suddenly, here was this new notion that there was no such thing as morality, so there was no reason to feel guilty or worry too much about others. For an idealistic teenager, reading Nietzsche felt a bit like getting kicked in the head.

So, the summer after my freshman year, I decided I'd personally prove Nietzsche wrong. Of course there was such a thing as morality! If you showed people unconditional love, I believed, they would reciprocate. Convinced my theory was true, I devised a way to test it: I walked out of my parents' house in Schenectady one June morning with just $20 in my pocket, and vowed not to return until I'd hitchhiked my way across the country. Hitchhiking, I thought, was the ultimate expression of trust. I would be putting myself at the mercy of total strangers, and I was excited at the prospect. The results of that trip would color my worldview forever.

I hitchhiked my way to New York City, walked through Harlem, slept in Central Park, and joined a peace march down to Washington, D.C. I sold turkey legs at a carnival booth in Virginia, went hiking in eastern North Carolina, caught rides with everyone from an older woman in a Karmann Ghia to rednecks in pickup trucks. Even as a dark-skinned, long-haired stranger in the rural South, I was almost always treated with respect and trust. I slept undisturbed under the stars. An optometrist I met at a diner in a town called Blowing Rock gave me the keys to his house, to stay there while he was away. And a student at Appalachian State University took me mountain climbing, which led to the most memorable experience of the trip—the experience that encapsulated exactly what I had set out to prove.

While we were mountain climbing, a spider bit me on my upper thigh. Over the next couple of days, the spot became swollen and tender, an angry red lump. It got so bad I feared I'd have to go to the emergency room—not an attractive option for a broke student with no health insurance card on him. I was calling my parents every week or so from pay phones, but they were worried enough as it was; I couldn't stand the thought of telling them I was suffering from an infected spider bite, too.

So I pressed on, catching a ride with a heavy-set, dark-haired guy outside Asheville, North Carolina. I slung my backpack into the backseat of his dark green Buick and started making small talk as we sped down the highway. After a while, I mentioned the mountain climbing—and the bite on my thigh.

To my surprise, he immediately pulled the Buick over to the side of the highway. "See those leaves over there?" he asked, pointing a burly finger. "Go grab a handful."

What should I do? If I got out, this stranger could just drive off with my backpack, leaving me helpless by the side of the road. But if I grabbed my backpack before getting out, he would know I didn't trust him, and the fragile bond we'd begun to establish would be broken. This was exactly the kind of moment that I'd come on the trip to experience—the kind of moment that could prove or disprove my theory. After a moment's hesitation, I opened the door and got out.

As I'd hoped, and even dared believe, the man stayed put. I grabbed a handful of the leaves, got back in the Buick, and we continued down the road. But that wasn't the end of the adventure.

We exited the highway, drove past a small town and soon ended up in an even more remote area. He turned down a dirt road and took me deeper into the woods, finally stopping in front of a modest one-story house with a couple of battered vehicles parked in front. The house was run-down, even foreboding. *Oh, boy*, I thought, *Here we go*. Nobody had any idea where I was; I was completely at the mercy of this man. Now I felt the stirrings of real fear.

We walked into the house, and the man went straight to the kitchen. A few minutes later, he came out and said to me, "OK, drop your shorts."

Every corpuscle in my body told me to run. But this was it: the ultimate test. Would my trust be repaid with trust? I dropped my shorts. And this big, burly, backwoods man took a few steaming leaves from a boiling pot and pressed them to the swollen lump on my thigh. A chemical property in the heated leaves sucked out the eggs the spider had laid there after its bite. Within a day, the sore had healed.

This experience, strange as it may sound, made a huge impression on me. It solidified my belief that putting out love and trust into the world is ultimately repaid in kind. And that belief became a cornerstone of what I've tried to do in India. While it's true that my good fortune on the road was partly the luck of the draw, I still believe there's a fundamental level at which trust is repaid with trust—and anyone who's ever experienced the kindness of a stranger knows exactly what I mean.

At every level, the work we do in India requires trust: we have to trust our borrowers to repay unsecured loans.

The borrowers have to trust others in their group to make payments, as no one receives a new loan unless everyone makes her payment. Our lenders have to trust that we'll protect their funds. And our investors have to trust that we'll steward their money in a way that will bring returns. Trust is the essential element of everything we do, and I learned it that summer while hitchhiking.

Back at Tufts, I continued studying philosophy and pondering how to get back to India after graduation. I spent my summers seeking out new experiences—working as a carnie in Canada, selling soda at Albany Yankees games, volunteering with Meals on Wheels. And I continued to explore the question of morality in my senior thesis, "Why Be Moral?"

Ultimately, it was the philosopher Thomas Hobbes who helped me reconcile the idealistic notions of being moral with the hard-core realities of everyday life. Hobbes, who famously wrote that life in the state of nature is "solitary, poor, nasty, brutish and short," believed that acting morally was not just a question of fulfilling an ethical obligation. It had a more prosaic, and more important, purpose: acting morally helped bring about a stable, functioning society. Moral guilt was useful, as it created a sense of responsibility toward others.

This wasn't some mushy philosophical theory. This was the perfect intersection of realism and idealism. And the fact that these two notions could coexist side by side was a revelation for me. It was the root of realizing that ethics didn't have to trump everyday living; it could complement and enhance it. Doing good and doing well could, and in fact should, coexist. This idea would later form the root of SKS.

As I finished my studies at Tufts, I was excited to get out into the world and test my theories. At long last, it was time to go to India and start working with the poor! The only problem was, I had no idea what I might do there, or who would hire a fresh-faced college graduate like me. And in those pre-Internet days, these questions were far more difficult to answer.

I went to the women's center on campus, knowing that groups working specifically with women were more progressive. I began flipping through magazines in hopes of finding a nonprofit located in drought-prone Telangana, the impoverished region of my birth. Because I spoke rudimentary Telugu and had family there, I figured that would be the best place to start. Unfortunately, there weren't as many options there as in cities like Delhi, Mumbai, or Kolkata, but eventually I tracked down the contact information for a few nonprofits. I sent off a raft of letters and waited.

Only one organization, the Deccan Development Society, responded. And even their letter was decidedly lukewarm. The director, a man named Biksham Gujja, basically said, "Okay, if you come here we'll meet with you, but we're not promising anything."

Relieved to have gotten a reply, and determined to convince Biksham to hire me, I bought a one-way plane ticket to Hyderabad and packed a single gym bag with clothes. I wanted to travel like Mahatma Gandhi—no unnecessary attachments, no excess of material goods. I had read about Gandhi's experiences in South Africa as a young man, when he was first developing his ideas, and I wanted to experience that same kind of awakening. And I knew I couldn't do it sitting in an academic environment in America.

So, this was it—I was finally going to India to help the poor! I was excited and a little nervous. I would have been more so if I'd known what a rude awakening awaited me on the other end.

CHAPTER TWO

Putting the Last First

"VIKRAM," said the man sitting across the table from me. "You cannot help the poor. So don't even try to approach it that way."

After four flights and twenty-four hours in transit from Schenectady, New York, to Hyderabad, one day to get used to the time change, and a nervous Monday morning auto-rickshaw trip across town, I'd finally made it to the offices of the Deccan Development Society—the only nonprofit that had responded to my letters. I had come on a mission, but here in my very first meeting, Biksham Gujja was shooting it down.

Biksham was DDS's director, a calm, laconic man with a thick mustache and a head of thinning hair. He'd seen my type before: eager young American, coming to India expecting to change the world. In his experience, most young people, no matter how dedicated they believed themselves to be, ended up moving on to other things when faced with the reality of working in India's poorest rural areas.

"The poor know a lot more than we do about how to help themselves," Biksham went on. "We're not all that much use to them, in that sense."

I heard Biksham's words, but I didn't believe what he was saying. Of course we could help the poor! We could teach them how to improve their lives. I could get access to information on new, more modern agricultural techniques, or study scientific dairying procedures, and go out into the villages and teach people what I'd learned. The poor obviously needed us! They were uneducated, and we were in a position to bring them knowledge.

I assumed Biksham was just being modest, as DDS had been working with India's poor for about seven years by then. Their work included agricultural programs, immunization drives, and other social projects, and they had established a thriving set of women's groups that met regularly in the region where DDS worked, a few hours' drive outside Hyderabad. So I just brushed aside his comment, and asked again whether I could volunteer with DDS.

"Sure," he said, a half-smile on his face. "Be ready at 6:30 a.m. tomorrow. We'll go out into the field, and I'll show you what we do."

THE NEXT MORNING I was up and ready to go, excited at the prospect of traveling to remote villages and meeting the people I hoped to serve. Biksham picked me up, and we made our way through the streets of Hyderabad just as the sun peeked over the rooftops and the traffic started flowing. We drove to the city's outskirts, then continued on a long, straight highway out of town.

There's a stark beauty to the Telangana countryside. It's extremely dry, so there are long stretches of dusty roads, yellowed brush, and withered, knotty trees. The earth in some areas is a deep red color, rich in iron. Tiny villages dot the landscape, and rutted dirt roads snake off into the odd copse of trees. The occasional roadside stand offers fresh fruits or cold drinks. And as you get farther and farther from the city, the air gets clearer and the sky bluer.

The roads in rural India are much rougher than those in the West, with potholes, accidents, and the occasional intrusion of farm animals slowing traffic. It took us about three hours to cover the ninety miles, but we finally pulled up to a collection of warm red mud-brick buildings in the center of a small village. "This is DDS headquarters," Biksham said. We got out of the car and I took a look around.

The DDS buildings were impressive, stately almost, amid the modest dun-colored village huts with thatched roofs. A tamarind tree stood sentry, giving shade, and a large well had been dug for fresh water. The main buildings were a couple of stories tall, with ornate mud-brick carvings and balconies overlooking the courtyards, and they were well kept and inviting. We walked into one, and Biksham began showing me around.

A large hand-painted map hung in the front hallway, dividing nearby villages into clusters. A small office off to one side was crammed to the ceiling with dusty ledgers, stacks of paper, folders—a forest's worth of paperwork. Straight ahead was a cavernous meeting room, its white-washed walls and open windows giving it a bright, open air. And seated on the floor in the room was a group of about forty women, all of whom began nodding and greeting Biksham as soon as we walked in.

"This is our village leaders group," Biksham told me, then gestured for me to sit down with them. "Have a seat," he said. "Observe."

I sat among the women, and they started their meeting; they obviously had been waiting for us to arrive. The first thing they did was sing a song—a simple tune, in unison, that opened each meeting. Though my Telugu was rusty, and the women's village dialect was different from what I was used to, I could make out the theme of the song: unity, the poor banding together to help each other.

Looking around the room at these women in their bright saris, their voices reverberating off the bare walls in the morning sun, I felt almost overwhelmed. This, I thought, is exactly where I want to be. I must have had a goofy, dreamy grin on my face when the song ended and Biksham spoke up. "This is Vikram," he said, gesturing to me. "He's going to spend some time with us. You all need to teach him Telugu."

The women laughed, and I looked around sheepishly. The challenge had been laid. Would I be disciplined enough to really learn Telugu? Could I take living in a remote village—away from television, telephones, newspapers, English-speaking friends, restaurants, and all the other comforts of home? Biksham clearly didn't think so, but later that day he showed me to a spartan dormitory-style room in the compound, and invited me to spend the night—and as many nights as I liked.

That whole first week, I watched and learned. I wanted to have a specific job to do, but that wasn't how Biksham operated. He wanted to see how I would comport myself with everyone, what I'd be drawn to, how I would spend my time. So, I just tagged along with others wherever I could. I hitched a ride with one DDS worker, Raghu, as he rode his motorbike out to check on an organic agricultural project, and we got drenched in a sudden downpour on the way back. I spent time at the DDS children's center, practicing my Telugu with the kids who'd drop by after school.

And I went to a night meeting in one village with another DDS employee named Ranga, which gave me my first taste of what to expect while working with villagers.

I suppose I'd expected poor village women to be docile and easily led. I had an image of women nodding deferentially, looking to us for help, gratefully accepting whatever wisdom we could impart. This was ridiculously, completely, embarrassingly wrong. When I went with Ranga to the village meeting, I saw just how ambitious and aggressively outspoken the women really were. If they didn't like something, they let you know right away. And they would not countenance being talked down to. It was fascinating to watch Ranga interact with the women. Very quickly, my stereotypic notions were being stripped away.

At the end of that first week, I heard DDS was starting a new immunization program. This entailed sending volunteers and workers out to villages, where they'd knock on doors and ask whether the children of the house had been immunized. It was a straightforward task, with a simple set of standard questions—the perfect opportunity for me to get involved. I asked Biksham if I could work on the immunization project, and to my relief, he said yes.

For the next month, I rode around to the surrounding villages in a jeep, working on both the immunization project and a DDS organic agriculture project. I spent time with community organizers, seeing how they worked, and got to know the rhythm of rural life. On occasion, if I was out late at night, I would stay over in the hut of a village family. I drank chai in village stalls, ate in small roadside dhabas and talked and listened as much as I could. I slept in my small bedroom at DDS and ate the community meals at the compound. The more I did, the more I wanted to do— there weren't enough hours in the day to have all the conversations and see all the sights I was drawn to.

At the end of that first month, Biksham decided I was doing enough to warrant a salary. I hadn't asked for one, and I knew DDS didn't have any extra funds floating around, but Biksham came up to me one afternoon and said, "We're going to pay you a thousand rupees a month for your work." I was thrilled at his vote of confidence, but when I told my grandmother in Hyderabad about it, she punctured my bubble quickly.

"I pay my watchman more than that," she said, and shook her head.

I wasn't surprised at her lack of enthusiasm—a thousand rupees was the equivalent of about $55 in 1990. But quite by accident, I soon discovered another reason why she, and my mother, were so dismayed at my new choice of profession.

AFTER I STARTED LIVING at the DDS compound, I'd occasionally travel back to Hyderabad to visit with my grandparents, aunts, and uncles. In fact, whenever I was there, I stayed at the same aunt's house where I'd seen the woman pick up those grains of rice all those years ago.

On one visit, I happened to read a newspaper article about one of my uncles, V. Hanumantha Rao, who was then in the running for chief minister of the state of Andhra Pradesh, where Hyderabad is located. A charismatic grass-roots politician with a deep, commanding voice, this uncle was close to former prime minister Rajiv Gandhi, son of the slain prime minister Indira Gandhi, and was considered an up-and-coming young Turk in Indian politics.

But what caught my eye was a piece of information I'd never heard before: my uncle—my whole family, in fact—came from a "backward" caste. This was a significant detail in the story, as historically, members of backward castes had only been allowed to undertake manual labor or serve as craftspeople. Those strict prohibitions had begun breaking down, but even my uncle and father's generation had had limited educational and career opportunities—and those were the result of affirmative action programs. Backward caste members were not historically politicians—or surgeons or philosophers or even NGO workers. In fact, they were the lowest in the four-tier Indian system, higher only than the Dalits, or untouchables.

The caste system is an ancient and enduring part of Indian society, set forth in sacred Hindu texts and long enshrined in the culture. There are four castes: the Brahmins, who are priests and scholars; the Kshatriyas, who are warriors and nobility; the Vaishyas, who are the merchant class; and the Shudras—the so-called backward caste—who are the laborers and tradespeople. Below all these are the "scheduled" caste, the untouchables, so named because the British government "scheduled" them for affirmative action programs as the era of British rule came to an end. Yet even today, members of the scheduled caste suffer horrific discrimination, including physical and psychological abuse, for their social position. Untouchables are still considered by some Indians to be subhuman, and are at times treated as such, being threatened, beaten, forced to humiliate themselves publicly, and sometimes even murdered simply for their status.

The system is deeply rooted in Indian consciousness, and although India's constitution makes it illegal to discriminate according to caste, the reality is that it happens all the time. It is a shamefully prejudicial way of dividing people, and the Indian government has tried to mitigate it over the years with affirmative action–style programs for members of backward and scheduled castes, in an effort to reverse the effects of centuries of discrimination.

I had always believed we were Vaishyas, or the merchant caste, as I knew my grandfather had run his own sari shop. Stunned by the revelation in the newspaper article, I asked him about it. And that was the first time I learned of my own family's struggle to overcome poverty.

As it turned out, my grandfather had indeed started out as a laborer. Born in 1916 in a village outside of Hyderabad, he was left fatherless at age three when my great-grandfather died, leaving him and his mother in a precarious economic position. Not able to cope alone, they moved from their village to Hyderabad city to stay with relatives. And although my great-grandmother found work at a general store run by a family member, she earned just 4 rupees per month—about $6 in today's terms, barely enough for them to survive. So my grandfather was forced to drop out of school in the fourth grade to work.

He started working as an errand boy in a cloth shop, earning a monthly salary of 50 *paisa*, roughly 75 cents. But my grandfather wasn't satisfied with the life that society, culture, and centuries of history had dictated for him. Ambition burned in him, and he began plotting his move out of poverty. He learned everything he could about textiles and the customers who came into the store, and eventually he worked his way up to salesman.

By the time he turned fifteen, he had developed a real knack for sales, helped along by his warm and affable nature. He managed to land a job at a different textile store at a higher salary, this time earning 3 rupees a month, about $4.50. Yet despite the raise, this was still not enough money to survive. So at sixteen, he took an additional job, working part time in the private army of the Nizam, the head of the traditional ruling dynasty of the Hyderabad region. He'd leave before dawn to go to the palace grounds, then get to the store by late morning and work into the night. The days were long and arduous: at age sixteen, my grandfather was working twelve to fourteen hours a day, six days a week.

Despite this rigorous pace, my grandfather kept trying to learn as much as possible about the textile business, even traveling with the shop manager to Mumbai to purchase saris. At the age of nineteen, he was ready to make his move: he asked the shop owner if he could start his own business. Not having any start-up capital, my grandfather proposed taking saris on credit, bicycling through neighborhoods, and selling them door to door. The owner agreed, and my grandfather quickly built up a loyal base of customers. Finally, in 1942, at age twenty-six, he was able to forge a partnership with a financier and start his own sari shop, Prabhat Cloth stores in Hyderabad's Sultan Bazaar. At the time, this was an amazing leap for a member of a backward caste.

My father grew up seeing the example of my grandfather's ambition. He, too, wanted to break the chains of our cultural heritage, and with the advent of affirmative action–style programs for lower castes in the fifties and sixties, he was able to push ahead even further. After my father finished high school, he studied medicine—the first person in our family to reach such heights in education. And when he became a doctor, he took the first opportunity he could to move to the United States, where he and my mother could raise a family in a society that didn't care what caste we came from.

The leap my own family took, in just two generations, was astonishing. It was emblematic of the changes taking place in India during that time. It was also the reason why my mother, Padma, in particular, was aghast at the career choice I was now making. She simply could not understand why, when she and my father had struggled so hard to create a better life for us in America, I would ever want to come back to live in a village and work with dirt-poor people in India. She was confused and disappointed, and she didn't hesitate to tell me so.

In fact, the first time she and my father came to visit after I started working with DDS, she not only told me exactly how she felt about it, she showed me—in a most unexpected way.

My parents had flown into Hyderabad, and I was eager to take them out into the field and show them the work I was doing. I had been in India about two months then, and I was proud of my progress: my Telugu was improving, I was learning the rhythms of village life, and I had many friends, colleagues, and DDS members I wanted them to meet. So we headed out to the villages, my mother reluctantly climbing into the jeep for the three-hour trip.

When we arrived at the DDS compound, I took my parents into the meeting hall, where several of the older women I'd become close to had gathered. This was a big moment for me—I was excited to introduce my mom to the women who were more or less my mother figures here in India. As a sign of respect, the women all sat on the floor and offered my mom the only chair in the room. This was a typical gesture, but my mother was mortified: it was obvious to everyone that she was fighting back tears. Why would her son choose this place, moving backward to poverty when there was so much promise elsewhere?

My mother tried to compose herself, and though I hoped they didn't pick up on the real source of her distress, the truth is that poor people know better than anyone when they're being judged. Yet the women were absolutely gracious, with one, Narsamma, offering a gentle running commentary to try to break the tension.

"What mother wouldn't be upset when her son goes far away?" she asked, smiling. "Of course, she misses Vikram. Of course she wants him near her." The other women offered up similar banalities, until mercifully it was time to take my parents into the villages.

Unfortunately, out in the field things got worse rather than better. I walked my parents around a couple of villages, introducing them to people I'd been working with and proudly showing off my language skills. It was a brutally hot day, which I apparently hadn't taken into account, because all of a sudden my mother keeled over and dropped to the dirt with a thud.

My god! I thought. *What have I done to my mother!* I knelt beside her and put my hand on her face. "Mom!" I shouted. "Are you okay?" At which point my physician father piped up.

"Ah, she's just fainted," he said. "Give her some water. She'll be fine."

The combination of sun and emotion had gotten to my mother, but my father actually seemed to be enjoying the field visit. He didn't say it in so many words, but I think he was proud of me. Though he's a surgeon, he's not your typical wealthy doctor—in part because, before he retired, he always voluntarily treated indigent patients, never refusing to see people just because they couldn't pay. He also volunteered at a local community center, and treated prisoners in his practice—I remember occasionally seeing big men in orange jumpsuits when I went to his office. My younger brother and I learned what it means to have a community ethic by watching my father at work. For my brother, that ethic translated into teaching high school in Beirut, Lebanon; for me, it meant coming back to India.

We managed to revive my mother, and soon got her and my father on the road back to Hyderabad. This was probably best, as very soon I would make a move into an even more remote part of India—a place where no one else in DDS would volunteer to go.

A COUPLE OF MONTHS into my stay at the DDS compound, Biksham told the employees that we'd gotten funding to expand into forty more villages. He wanted someone to head up this new program, but the person would have to move to a tiny speck of a village in an even more poverty-stricken area.

Though my mother had been unimpressed, the DDS compound actually had many comforts—a staff of women who cooked communal meals, a continuous schedule of meetings and activities, and the children's center, to name just a few. And although it was located in a small village, the compound wasn't far from a larger town, which at least had a couple of restaurants and even a movie theater. This new assignment, by contrast, would involve moving to an area that was not only miles away, but lacked basic modern conveniences like running water and reliable electricity. And none of the DDS employees who were qualified to run the program had any desire to take it on.

To me, it sounded like heaven. "I'll do it," I told Biksham. "I'd like to run this project."

Biksham sized me up. Over the last couple of months, I had proven I was committed to working in rural India. I'd done everything he asked of me. And now I was asking for more. Besides—no one else would do it, so what choice did he have? "Okay, Vikram," he said. "Here's your opportunity."

I had arrived in India with only my gym bag of clothes, but the women at DDS weren't about to let me go off into the sticks without some essentials. They quickly rounded up pots and pans, a few dishes, some utensils and basic tools, and sheets and a pillow. A DDS driver and I loaded everything in the back of a jeep, and off we went.

Eventually, the driver rolled to a stop in front of a small, abandoned two-room building in the middle of a huge field. "Here we are!" he said. As I got out I saw where "here" was: essentially, the middle of nowhere. He helped me unload my things, and together we carried them into the small room that would serve as my new home.

The first thing I noticed was that there was no door—meaning no way to keep out mosquitoes and flies, wandering animals, or other intruders. The second thing was that this was the most austere room imaginable. There was nothing in it; the walls were utterly bare, and there weren't even windows to speak of. Parched fields stretched around me in every direction, and in the distance there was a rock quarry. There was no one around, though a small village was visible in the distance.

The driver walked me to the village and introduced me to a few locals. In any rural Indian village, word spreads quickly when something unusual happens—or, as in this case, when someone unusual shows up. Soon enough, a small group had gathered, asking what I was doing there. "I'm from the Deccan Development Society," I told them. "We're starting a new project in your area."

Most were simply curious, though one man seemed concerned for my safety. "I will stay here with you until you get a door," he said. I was grateful, but also felt a little silly. Here I was trying to head up a big new project, and I was being looked after like a little boy. It was mildly embarrassing—but it was hardly the last time I'd end up feeling embarrassed in this village.

As I quickly learned, I pretty much didn't know how to do anything I needed to do. The man who'd volunteered to stay with me ended up helping me build a small fire, so I could at least boil some water and make some rice and dal for dinner. But where would I get water? There was obviously no running water in my little room, and I had no clue where the nearest well was. He walked me to the well and showed me how to draw water. And when I asked about where to use the bathroom, he gestured to the vast field.

"There's a quarry down the way," he said. "Just go down there. Everyone does." As it turned out, the little building that would serve as my new home was originally part of a weighing station for trucks headed to and from the quarry. After excavation there had stopped, the weighing station was abandoned, and it had sat unused since that time. The first thing I needed to do was get some doors made—but how do you go about that in a village you've never been to, with no obvious way to find out? Fortunately, a DDS staff person lived in a village nearby, and Biksham told him to stop by to help me out. Within a week, he helped me get some doors made.

The other person who helped me out was the village "fixer"—a local resident who acts as a dealmaker and general conduit between those who need something and those who can provide it. The first thing the fixer did was find a woman to cook for me. I had never imagined I'd have my own cook, but the reality was, it was just too time-consuming to have to gather firewood, make a fire, haul water to boil, and prepare food every day. I had no refrigerator or icebox, so everything had to be made fresh. The simple process of existing consumed far more energy and time than I had ever imagined.

Anyone who thinks poor people are lazy should spend a week living as they do. With none of the conveniences the developed world takes for granted, every chore takes inordinate amounts of time and energy. From cooking to bathing to cleaning, nothing was easy. And I found that, embarrassingly, I had no clue how to do the simplest things.

"No, no, no!" the local women yelled the first time they saw me trying to wash my clothes. They explained the process to me: First, soak your clothes with either soap powder or a hard soap cake. You do it by the well, so the water will run off in drainage. Then, you wring out the sudsy water and whack each item hard against the well stones, to get the dirt out. Finally, you rinse the clothes, tie them together, and hang them off a nearby tree. I didn't want to admit it, but the first few times I washed my clothes, I was sore the next day from the exertions.

Even more embarrassing was learning how to use the bathroom, village-style. As I'd been told, I would need to head down to the quarry and just find a place to go. But Indians, unlike Westerners, don't use toilet paper—they simply bring a small pot of water and use their left hand (hence the intense cultural taboo against ever eating with your left hand, or offering it in a social setting). Unfortunately, until I got the hang of it, I needed to bring a good deal more water out to the quarry, which led to snickers from villagers whenever I passed by with my small bucket of water.

I also set about trying to dig a well. We were hoping to turn the old weighing station into another DDS compound, and also had a plan to reforest the land surrounding it, so we'd need a closer source of water than the existing well. What did I know about digging a well? Nothing—that wasn't something they taught at Tufts. So I decided to hire a local laborer to help me do it. I had someone in mind, but had no idea what such a job should pay. And unfortunately, such a direct question will never result in a direct answer in an Indian village. "How much should I pay him?" I asked a few locals. "Well," they would reply, wobbling their heads in a common Indian gesture, "You know how much!" I didn't, but I decided to wing it. So I hired several more laborers, both men and women, to get the project going. The men would use the pickaxes and shovels, slowly descending into the deepening hole, and the women would haul the dirt away. They dug and scraped and sweated, toiling for hours in the hot sun until finally hitting bedrock, at which point I hired a couple of guys to come in with dynamite to finish the job. They blew the bedrock to smithereens, and the laborers descended even further down to cart out the rubble. Soon, we had made a giant, gaping hole, deep enough to require carving a set of steps to get out.

It was incredibly impressive. And dry as a bone.

I felt disappointed, even a little silly. But fortunately, Biksham had given me an extremely valuable piece of advice when he'd sent me off into the hinterlands.

"Don't worry about making a mistake," he'd told me. "It'll be okay. Just do what you think is best."

I really had no other choice, since there was no telephone in the village, and I had no way of checking in with Biksham to debate my decisions, large or small. Every other week or so, I'd ride my Hero Honda motorbike back to DDS headquarters to meet with Biksham and give him updates on the project, but other than that, I just had to make decisions based on my not-so-vast twenty-one years of life experience. It was extremely helpful to know I wouldn't be criticized in the inevitable event that something went wrong.

In the meantime, I was starting to understand what Biksham meant when he said, "You cannot help the poor." India was rife with well-intended but badly conceived projects that misguided elites had inflicted on the poor.

Bureaucrats gave subsidized loans so the poor could buy high-milk-yielding buffaloes—but the buffaloes couldn't handle drought conditions and died. A project that introduced capital-intensive agriculture led to a drop in the water tables, so although a handful of farmers benefited, everyone else in the community suffered. Educational programs for poor children failed to prepare them for the formal economy, but succeeded in alienating them from their traditional economies, leaving them ill-equipped for either situation., In fact, it seemed that most efforts to "help" the poor ended up harming them in some way instead.

There was a strikingly wide gap between the conversations I had with educated Indians in Hyderabad and the Indians I knew in the villages. And the longer I spent in the field, the clearer it became that the people who knew most about how to help the poor were the poor themselves. It made me wonder why those in a position to help always seemed to avoid asking those they wished to help what they truly needed.

Around this same time, I began reading a book called *Rural Development: Putting the Last First*, by Robert Chambers. Its central point was that the development community takes a top-down view of rural poverty, with NGO executives and bureaucrats getting their information from either large-scale survey questionnaires or brief and hurried visits to villages located just outside of cities. Because they have limited direct engagement with poor people, they get incomplete information, so they end up designing inadequate, and sometimes downright harmful, programs. Poor people themselves are actually far more knowledgeable about their situations than outsiders, and they also have ideas about how to improve things.

As a liberal college student, I had bought into the notion that the poor aren't terribly knowledgeable, and that they need education from outsiders. But from my experience of living in Indian villages, I quickly realized that they generally knew far more than I did. During my first few months in the village, I was the one always looking for help, support, and ideas from them, not the other way around.

Putting the Last First forever changed the way I approached the poor. It was the final piece of the puzzle; reading that book while simultaneously watching the poor in their own environment convinced me that Biksham was absolutely right. We couldn't help the poor—but what we could do, and had to do, was help the poor to help themselves. Every product, every system, every program that was designed to help the poor had to be designed by the poor themselves. This became my new goal.

I also came to one more, equally important realization at this time. No matter what I was doing at DDS headquarters or in the villages—immunization, agricultural initiatives, health, education, whatever—the conversation always came back around to the same thing: money.

I began noticing that, whenever I'd go to a village to talk about launching a DDS initiative, there would be a brief flurry of conversation among the village leaders. As my language skills improved, I could glean what these conversations were about: people were discussing who I was, and what I was in the village to do. Was I the guy who could give out microloans? No? Then who was?

Villagers cared about social projects such as educational and health initiatives, but only to a point. What they really wanted was loans for entrepreneurial activities. They wanted to be able to take care of themselves; everything else was secondary.

This was a huge revelation for me—the second one I'd had since coming to India. Now I knew these two things: first, that the poor must control their own ascent from poverty. And second, that money was the root of all self-empowerment solutions. Now the question became, how could I bring these two ideas together to help eliminate poverty?

I wanted to stay in India and keep searching for the answer, but after more than a year in the field, Biksham gave me a piece of advice. "You should go back to America," he said. "You will burn out if you stay here. Go back and get a graduate degree."

He was right. Living in India was exhilarating but exhausting. With reluctance, I returned to the United States to continue my studies, counting the days until I could return to the villages. By the time I returned three years later, I knew the answer of how to meld these two powerful ideas: microfinance.

What I didn't yet realize was that microfinance, as it was then practiced, still wouldn't be enough.

CHAPTER THREE

The Story of My Experiments with Grameen

IN THE FALL of 1974, when I was a boy happily playing soccer in Schenectady, a man named Muhammad Yunus was watching a catastrophe unfold in his native Bangladesh. Famine had struck the land, and hundreds of thousands of people were suffering, and dying, for lack of food.

Yunus, then a thirty-four-year-old economist, had gotten his PhD at Vanderbilt and had stayed active in Bangladeshi politics even while living in the United States. But in 1974, he returned to Bangladesh, where he joined the faculty of Chittagong University to teach economics. That fall, his fate—and the fate of millions of poor people—changed forever when Yunus, moved by the plight of a group of starving families, gave a $27 loan to help them launch a small business to get them out of poverty. It was a minuscule amount by Western standards, but a lifeline for his starving compatriots. And it sparked an idea.

Within two years, Yunus launched an experiment: a project to determine the feasibility of offering very small loans to very poor people, to help them out of poverty. He started in a village called Jobra, and quickly expanded to other nearby villages. What he found was that not only were poor Bangladeshis eager to start their own enterprises, they were surprisingly good at it, too. The project, called Grameen, from the Bengali word for "villages," continued to expand.

By 1983, the Grameen experiment was spreading like wildfire, with more and more Bangladeshis clamoring for loans. That year, the Bangladeshi government granted the Grameen project official bank status, and the newly incorporated Grameen Bank continued to expand. Over the next two decades, Grameen would reach more than 7 million borrowers, handing out more than $6 billion in loans. Grameen Bank wasn't the first-ever microfinance institution (MFI), but it was certainly the most influential, as new MFIs that cropped up in the ensuing years often borrowed its innovative practices. For his vision and effort in spreading the practice of microfinance, Yunus was awarded the Nobel Peace Prize in 2006.

Muhammad Yunus was already a legend when I began studying microfinance in the early 1990s. I had read all about him and thought what he was doing was incredibly visionary. And after spending a year in remotest India, seeing how entrepreneurial and energetic the villagers really were, I realized that I wanted to do what Yunus was doing. Microfinance was the key; it gave poor people the power to help themselves, rather than bestowing misguided help on them from above. My next foray to India was a perfect example of this.

I had returned to the United States at Biksham's urging to embark on graduate studies, but for the whole three years in the States, I was plotting a return to India. My studies were a bit haphazard—I bounced from Harvard to the World Watch Institute to a master's program at Yale— but I was fortunate enough to win a Fulbright Scholarship in 1994, enabling me to return to DDS and the villages. The new project I'd be working on demonstrated exactly how misguided programs designed to "help" the poor could be updated and improved.

In the early 1990s, the Indian government had set up a food grain distribution program. Essentially, the state would buy grain and give it to people at a subsidized cost. It was a well-intentioned project, but not very practical in terms of sustainability, as the money flow was all one-way, from the government to the people.

So DDS came up with an alternative. Instead of simply using the subsidy to give poor people grain, why not give them that same subsidy money as a no-interest loan? Then they could plant and grow their own grain, sell some of it and keep some for themselves, and repay the government its money. This would be far more sustainable than the existing program—and on top of it all, it would also create jobs for agricultural field workers and regenerate lands left fallow for lack of capital.

The government agreed with DDS, and funded the project to the tune of $250,000. And I was offered the chance to head it up. This would be my first time working on a project that was purely about microfinance, and I was excited. What I didn't anticipate was that the new program, well-intentioned as it was, was a bit of a mess.

I recruited several loan officers to help me cover the thirty villages. Their task was theoretically simple: set up meeting times in each village, then travel there at the appointed times to hand out loans, collect repayments, and discuss any problems with borrowers. In reality, it became a nightmare.

Some borrowers repaid their loans in grain, but for those who repaid in cash, several problems arose. For one thing, the various people who'd received loans had different schedules for repaying. Some were supposed to make payments periodically throughout the growing season, while others made a lump-sum payment at the end of the season. And because these were zero-interest loans, provided with government subsidies, some borrowers didn't seem terribly concerned about repaying at all.

Meetings in villages were typically scheduled for evenings and nights. A loan officer would ride his motorbike into a village, sometimes with a backpack full of cash—either from previous repayments or for new loans. It wasn't safe to be carrying that much cash at night, but there wasn't really an alternative, as the agricultural work the loans were paying for had to take place in daylight hours.

Because the loan repayments were all in differing amounts, each loan officer had to keep careful track of who paid how much, counting out crumpled bills and sorting through handfuls of coins, then writing the varying numbers down in a ledger. He'd then record the amounts in a receipt for each borrower, again writing everything by hand, on the spot, as there weren't standard preset amounts. The process wasn't automated at all—not in the field, and not back at DDS headquarters, where information from the ledgers was painstakingly hand-copied into other ledgers, and stored in giant stacks of books.

With thirty villages in our program, we were manually tracking thousands of transactions. And with differing amounts and differing dates of repayment for everyone, the process was far more complicated than it needed to be. But for the whole year and a half I headed the project, that was how we did it, even though one thought kept creeping into my head: there has to be a better way to do this. At the time, however, this was how everyone in microfinance kept track—by hand, in ledgers, with all the mistakes and inefficiencies that entailed.

And this still wasn't the biggest problem with microfinance. The biggest problem was revealed that summer, when I had to tell that determined, hopeful woman in the faded purple sari that we had no money to expand to her village. Her response—"Am I not poor, too?"—pushed me to the next level: I realized then that I didn't simply want to practice microfinance, I wanted to improve it. I wanted to make it possible for *everyone* who desired a loan to get one.

But how would that be possible? When I returned to my studies in the United States after eighteen months of running the DDS microfinance project, I resolved to answer that question once and for all.

O N RETURNING TO THE States in 1996, I enrolled in a PhD program at the University of Chicago. In reality, I didn't much care about getting a doctorate; I just wanted to have time to plot my move into full-time microfinance. Chicago was very strong in Indian studies, and it had an excellent political science department, so that's where I headed. Studying political science gave me the greatest latitude in finding a dissertation topic, but there was another reason why I chose it.

Although microfinance is, on the surface, about loans and business and interest rates, my time in India had convinced me that at its core it's really about power. Success in microfinance wasn't measured only in numbers. It was measured in the changing power dynamics. It was about changing historical and cultural norms, shifting centuries-old power structures in a way that would help the traditionally downtrodden. So a political science doctorate seemed a more natural fit for what I was trying to accomplish than, say, economics.

The more I thought about the problem of how to scale microfinance, the more I realized there were three essential problems with the way it was practiced. First, there was never enough money to go around—the problem I'd faced with the woman in the purple sari. Second, the haphazard way it was practiced, with differing loan amounts and dates of repayments, for example, made the process highly inefficient. And third, the cost of doing business was too high—with so many tiny loans, and so much time and energy required to collect on them, the transaction costs were too high and the margins too low to be sustainable.

I began to think of these problems as the "three *c*'s": capital, capacity, and costs. I didn't know yet how to solve them, but I believed that if I could, microfinance could expand to serve tens of millions—even hundreds of millions—more people than it was then serving. Yes, existing MFI's were doing a lot of good, but with 800 million poor people in India alone, "good" was never going to be good enough.

In the midst of all this pondering and planning and studying, I hit on a simple but powerful idea: why not make the practice of microfinance operate more like a business? A highly profitable business, which would generate income, sustain itself, and even make enough money to attract commercial capital? That way, the pot of money could continue to grow, even as more and more loans were given out.

Some other emerging microfinance leaders had similar ideas, but this notion of highly commercial microfinance was pretty radical for the time. There seemed to be an unspoken law that microfinance providers had to function as nonprofits—they could offer loans to the poor and charge interest, but only as much as they needed to cover the bare-bones minimum cost of supporting the work. Money for microcredit typically came from government grants or foundations or donors, and when it was lent out, it was gone. Sure, it eventually came back in the form of repayments, but there was no way to grow the programs beyond the number of people those finite donations could serve at any given time.

Turning microfinance into a commercial venture seemed to be the perfect solution. If a microfinance institution could be run as a profitable enterprise, it could attract investment from private investors—those who expected a return. Since private investors are a virtually unlimited pool—after all, everybody wants a return on their investments—there would be no limit on the amount of funding available. And inviting private investors would have another benefit: once we had the equity provided by their investments, commercial banks would be willing to lend us even more money, giving us a vastly bigger pool of capital. The only catch was that interest rates would have to be fair for borrowers but high enough to not only cover costs but provide investors a healthy return.

This seemed an acceptable trade-off to me. Why did "doing good" necessarily have to be a nonprofit activity? Why did the money flow have to be in only one direction, from donors to the poor? Why not bring the circle around, making it possible for donors—or investors, as the case would be—to make money from supporting microfinance? There was an artificial wall between nonprofit and for-profit ventures, but there didn't have to be. Did there?

I was excited about this idea, and started writing a business plan. The notion of actually starting a company was way too daunting—especially since I'd seen the level of bureaucracy and corruption I'd have to navigate in India—so initially, I just wanted to start an experimental for-profit branch of an existing MFI. I started pulling together funding proposals while still doing my PhD coursework, setting a crazy pace that, unbeknownst to me then, wouldn't slow down for more than a decade.

I didn't know anything about raising money, but my efforts got a jumpstart when the Chicago-based Indian Development Service, a volunteer group formed to support Indian NGOs, made me an offer. I had asked them for $10,000—more than their typical grants of $5,000 or so—and they said they'd give it to me, on one condition. I had to raise $10,000 from other sources to match it.

This instantly put me into high gear. With $20,000, my crazy idea just might become a reality. But where would I get the $10,000 to match their grant? I picked up the phone and started dialing people—colleagues of my father, friends of my mother, parents of my Indian friends, anyone who I thought might be willing to give a few dollars.

It was tough going at first. I had no idea what I was doing, and felt slightly cowed at asking people for money. I'd spend a half-hour on the phone with a wealthy Indian American doctor, listening to him pontificate about "what India needs," and then at the end he'd offer me $50. I went to an event my late uncle, Chandra Shekhar Thunga, put together at his house in Chicago, and when I felt too timid to ask for money outright, he pulled me aside and said, "Vikram, your idea is good. But you have no idea how to raise money from Indians. You have to say, 'Give me a check for $1,000 now!'" This wasn't the first time, nor would it be the last, that someone told me I needed to be more direct with Indians.

My parents stepped up, too, holding samosa-and-tea parties for friends so I could come and do my song and dance, complete with a slide presentation. Having seen my mother's reaction to my work in India, and knowing how much she wished I would pursue a different career, I was really touched by her show of support. With their help, the money continued to trickle in on my visits home to New York. People would hand me $51 or $101 at the end of a samosa evening (superstitious Indians never give an amount ending in zero, as it means the funding will end there). My parents also gave money, as did my uncle in Chicago, who pitched in $5,001 himself.

I also filled out applications for grants from foundations; this was another thing I'd never done before, so I sought some outside help. One afternoon in the spring of 1997, I made my way to the basement office of the university's associate dean of student services seeking guidance for writing these proposals. I walked into a modest room ringed with piles of paperwork—a typical no-frills student services office—and greeted the woman seated behind the desk. Her name was Michelle Obama.

At the time, Barack Obama was running for the Illinois state Senate, and Michelle had recently left her position with the nonprofit organization Public Allies. She was developing the university's Community Service Center, and she was the most accessible and knowledgeable adviser I could think of to ask for help.

Over the course of several meetings, she advised me on a proposal I was writing to the Echoing Green Foundation, giving me valuable feedback on drafts. She suggested that I offer more concrete details in my proposal, as I had a habit of telling the stories of the poor women I'd met, but sometimes fell short on enumerating what exactly I needed. "You need to be more specific," she told me. "How much money are you looking for in the first and second years? You need to work out your budget." With her help, I realized I needed to show the foundation that I knew what I was doing operationally, not just philosophically.

With all the fund-raising parties, grant applications, and coursework, the academic year passed by in a blur. I hit up everyone I knew, and donations trickled in from more than three hundred people, some of whom gave as little as $11. But by the end of the year, I had managed to raise about $52,000, including the $10,000 matching grant—far more than I had dreamed possible.

The next step was finding an existing microfinance institution that would let me open a for-profit branch as an experiment. This shouldn't be too hard, I thought, since I was bringing my own money to fund the project. But as I soon found out, money alone wasn't enough to break down the entrenched thinking among existing MFIs.

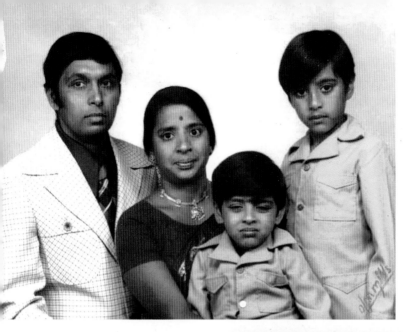

Top: With my parents and brother in the early 1970s: Akula Krishna, Padma Krishna, Gautham, and me. *Above:* With my mother in Hyderabad on my first birthday. *Right:* My grandfather, Akula Venkatramiah. Although a member of the "backward" caste, he worked his way up from laborer to shop owner.

Top: My home in Shamshuddinpur, the remote village where I led my first DDS project. My room had no door when I first moved in. *Above:* I learned to wash my clothes by hand at the well in Shamshuddinpur village.

Above: Sathamma, SKS's first member, poses in front of her thatched mud hut. Her first loan was for 1,000 rupees— about $25—to start a vegetable vending business. She eventually earned enough money to build a new house. *Left:* The unflappable S. Rama Laxmi, SKS's first employee.

Right, top: Looking at goats with SKS's second employee, Nirmala, and Rama, in the village of Islampur. They could tell when villagers tried to pass off one goat as another, even if I couldn't. *Right, bottom:* SKS's first branch office, and our Tata Sumo jeep, in Narayankhed town. We started off in one room on the second floor, and eventually expanded into almost the entire building.

Top: We eventually moved the Narayankhed branch office to a nearby village, Anthwar. I lived in this small building. This was also the room where a group of men carrying crowbars tried to attack Shyam Mohan, our new COO. Our branch staff is conducting a weekly meeting on the roof.

Right, top: In a center meeting I'm disbursing a loan for a borrower to purchase a milk-producing water buffalo. She milks the buffalo, keeps some milk for her family, and sells the rest, using the proceeds to pay off the loan in one year.

Right, bottom: Compulsory Group Training in Islampur, one of our first villages. We use visual group exercises to teach financial literacy, explaining to our members—most of whom are illiterate—our products and procedures. Here we're using cash and coins to explain the weekly repayments and interest rates.

Left, top: Using chalk powder, seeds, coins, and kernels of sorghum, a group of borrowers creates a seasonal cash-flow diagram. Based on this, we set our initial loan amounts, installment amounts, and frequency of payments.

Left, bottom: Each SKS village center—230,000 in all as of January 2010—elects a leader. These leaders meet annually in regional meetings to give feedback and suggestions to the SKS team and learn about new pilot products. Here they're voting on whether they like a new loan product we're designing.

Below: The part of my work I enjoy the most is attending center meetings. In this center in Hyderabad, I'm taking a poll of members who are receiving an SKS insurance product.

Right: The older SKS passbooks functioned in a paper-based system, though the company now has moved to a computer-based system.
Below: SKS has piloted a mobile banking initiative in which store owners and borrowers conduct all their transactions through mobile phones. The pilot project has run smoothly for a year, but regulatory changes are needed before we can roll it out on a larger scale.

Above: Rahul Gandhi, prominent Indian politician and the grandson of Indira Gandhi, attends a center meeting at Bandasomwaram village in Nalgonda district. I'm sitting to his left, and Praseeda Kunam, in red dress, is on his right. (D. Ravinder Reddy, Ravi Press Photo.) *Left:* With the pioneer of microfinance, Nobel Prize winner Muhammad Yunus. I have always considered Yunus a role model; prior to returning to India to start SKS, I spent two weeks at Grameen Bank, learning how they operate.

Above: SKS members use their loans to start all kinds of businesses. Here a woman shows off her cobbler business. *Below:* Another member runs a seamstress business, thanks to SKS loans.

. . .

IN EARLY FEBRUARY of 1997, the first-ever Microcredit Summit was held at the Sheraton in Washington, D.C. Three thousand people came from all over the world, and First Lady Hillary Rodham Clinton gave the keynote address. I knew Muhammad Yunus was going to be there, as well as the leaders of MFIs operating in India, so I packed up my only suit and tie and headed for the capital.

Despite having raised $52,000 for my project, I had no money myself, so I got into the summit by volunteering to be an official timekeeper for the sessions. As soon as the volunteer schedule came out, I jockeyed with the other timekeepers to get into the sessions I wanted. This was the perfect way to attend the conference for free, but unfortunately it was hard to approach the panelists as a colleague when they saw me as merely a student volunteer. However, this was my big chance, so I took every opportunity to tell others about my project.

I approached David Gibbons, who was launching a microfinance initiative called Cashpor in the Indian state of Uttar Pradesh. I talked to Udaia Kumar of Share MicroFin, which had been operating in India since 1989. I met Ela Bhatt of the Self-Employed Women's Association, or SEWA. I approached Alex Counts of the Grameen Foundation USA, as I couldn't even get close to Muhammad Yunus, who even then had a kind of rock-star status. I hustled and talked and introduced myself to everyone who I thought might be interested in my for-profit experiment.

Unfortunately, I was met with a cascade of no's. No one wanted to take a chance on an untested theory cooked up by an eager graduate student. I was told I was "too young," "not experienced enough," and in two cases, "too American" to make the project work. No matter how persuasively I argued, no matter how much I tried to charm my listeners, nothing worked. I left the summit disappointed and embarrassed that no one seemed to take me seriously. But I also felt the stirrings of something else: a determination to prove them all wrong.

If no one wanted to take a chance on me, then fine. I would do it myself! I hadn't planned to start my own organization, and didn't relish the idea of all the paperwork and bureaucratic hassle it would entail, but I believed so strongly in my idea that there was no other choice. I decided to call it SKS, for Swayam Krishi Sangam, a Sanskrit phrase meaning "self-work society", or more loosely, "self-help society"

I returned to Chicago feeling exhilarated and daunted. Raising money was one thing, but launching an independent organization—in India, no less—was quite another. I spent the rest of the spring and summer doing research, and asking as many people as possible for advice. Given its status as a pioneer in the field, I knew I wanted to follow the example of Grameen Bank. So in November of 1997, I traveled to Bangladesh for a two-week training session with Grameen.

The Grameen Dialogue program was designed for people who wanted to learn the Grameen system for distributing loans and collecting payments. Over the nearly two decades Grameen had been in business, its management had plenty of time to try out different methods and see what worked best. From what I saw in the field, the basics of their system were elegant and efficient, so I resolved to borrow their ideas for SKS.

Grameen lent almost exclusively to women, as men had proven more likely to spend cash in hand on personal items, rather than on their businesses or households. Also, women had shown themselves to be excellent entrepreneurs, despite cultural biases to the contrary. Putting women in charge of a household's loan was a way of empowering them, too, though that was a welcome by-product of the system rather than a goal of it.

The Grameen system was based on an ingenious combination of trust and peer pressure. Borrowers were divided into subgroups of five, and within a given village there might be as many as eight of these subgroups, making a total of forty borrowers. Each woman in the group was responsible for her own loan repayments, but if any one woman missed a payment, no one else in the group could receive a loan until it was paid.

In this way, all the women looked out for each other, and kept each other in line. They shared a community bond—a bond the weekly meetings were designed to strengthen. The women would gather each week at the appointed time, opening their meeting by reciting, in unison, a series of pledges—to follow the rules of the lending program, to look out for their fellow borrowers, to send their children to school, and so forth. And the Grameen loan officers would collect payments, approve new loans, and address any questions the borrowers had.

Sitting in on a borrowers' meeting is a powerful experience. Taking my place in the group, looking around at these entrepreneurial poor women in their colorful saris and bangles, I remembered the feeling I had on my first visit to DDS, seeing the village leaders sing. These meetings are the most basic building blocks for ending poverty: they represent poor people taking control of their own destinies, pulling themselves up and creating not only economic betterment, but hope for themselves. Seeing this in action is nothing short of inspiring.

It's easy, and common, to assume that poor people are not very smart. Why else would they still be mired in poverty, after all? But the truth is that huge numbers of poor people are both very smart and very entrepreneurial, as we've seen time and again in the microfinance world. The expression "a fistful of rice" even comes from an entrepreneurial practice of the poor: a woman cooking a pot of rice will typically take one handful of grains and put it away in a separate place. This "fistful of rice" is an investment, a hedge against possible shortages later.

The beauty of microfinance is that it provides tools for the poor that they've never had access to before. That lack of access has been devastating: it's like trying to play tennis without a racquet, or becoming a great musician without an instrument. No matter what innate talent you may have, it's useless without the simple tools needed to express or develop it. Over the years, Grameen's borrowers had launched all kinds of successful enterprises, from setting up small home-front stores to tailoring to potato farming to selling goat milk. People could choose to invest in something they were good at, rather than something that was dictated to them.

I took in everything I could during that two-week program, scribbling notes and asking numerous questions. The Grameen model would serve as a perfect basis for SKS, but I already saw a few things that needed changing. One particularly jarring example came when I asked a Grameen loan officer for a loan history of one of his members.

"Give me a day," the loan officer said.

I assumed he asked for some time because he was busy, but to my astonishment, he needed the time to pull down dusty ledgers from previous years, so he could look up and then scribble down by hand each loan and repayment this member had made. Imagine walking into any Western bank and asking for records pertaining to a clients' loans or deposits—no modern bank would have to page through handwritten ledgers to produce those figures. It was utterly primitive, shockingly so. From that moment, I knew we would have to find a way to automate our recordkeeping, even if it meant developing a new software program to do it.

At the end of the two-week session, I finally got to meet the man I thought of as a personal hero: Muhammad Yunus. He was the closing speaker for a small group of us, and afterward we all got a chance to spend a few minutes talking with him. I was excited at having the chance to meet him—and cocky enough to tell him I planned to improve upon his methods.

"You know how Gandhi called his autobiography *The Story of My Experiments with Truth*"? I asked him. "Well, one day I'm going to write my autobiography and call it *The Story of My Experiments with Grameen*." Yunus just smiled, no doubt amused at the hubris of this twenty-something upstart who had yet to distribute a single loan from his own organization.

Despite my seeming arrogance, I was starstruck enough that I bought three traditional handwoven Bangladeshi shirts from Grameen's borrower-run textile company, so I could dress like Yunus. I still have one of them—the other two wore out from overuse. And I also still have the small, intricately decorated hand-fan he gave to each of us, hand-made by one of Grameen's borrowers. Meeting Yunus was definitely a thrill, and I made no secret of wanting to emulate him. But I wanted to outperform him, too.

I N DECEMBER of 1997, shortly after finishing the Grameen program, I made my way from Bangladesh to Hyderabad. This was it: time to start SKS and get the ball rolling on what I was convinced would be a better, stronger, more efficient microfinance system. Unfortunately, the process of getting permission to bring my $52,000 into India would prove slower, less efficient, and more frustrating than I ever imagined.

I enlisted DDS cofounder Vithal Rajan as chairperson and went to register SKS as soon as I arrived in India. I ran into the first snag when a government official asked me for a bribe to complete the paperwork. This wasn't terribly surprising, as Indians have for centuries followed a tradition of handing out *baksheesh*, or small bribes, to get things done. But even though it's absolutely ingrained in the culture, and taken for granted by many Indians, I was determined not to grease anyone's palms for any reason. Whatever money I had was earmarked for the poor, and I resented the notion of paying extra for ordinary services.

So, instead of paying the bribe, I just kept coming back to the same office every day—day in and day out—until they at last got sick of seeing me and agreed to register SKS. That was step one.

Step two was transferring the $52,000 from the United States into India. The Indian government keeps close tabs on large sums of money that are transferred into and out of the country to ensure it isn't being used for terrorist activities or money laundering, so a fair amount of paperwork was required to make the transfer. Once again, an official asked me for a bribe to expedite getting permission, and once again I said no.

But this official was far more stubborn than the first. He knew how much money I was trying to bring in, so he knew the stakes were high. He had to assume that, with tens of thousands of dollars in the balance, I'd be willing to skim a little off the top to make things easier—that's just how things are done. But to his surprise, I refused to do it. And so we found ourselves at a stalemate.

Weeks went by. I kept pushing for permission, and he kept denying it. We met periodically, though neither of us would budge even slightly in the other's direction. I couldn't believe this—here I was, trying to bring money into a country that needed all the help it could get to alleviate poverty, and I was being met by a stony "No, thank you." This was ludicrous! It wasn't like I was trying to come in and take money from Indians—just the opposite. After all the work I'd done already, it was incredibly frustrating to be sitting in Hyderabad, waiting for permission that might never come.

After six weeks of failed cajoling, my resolve began to break down. I set up yet another meeting with the official, which again ended in a stalemate. He and I ended up sharing a three-wheeled auto-rickshaw taxi, zooming through Hyderabad on our way to our respective homes after the meeting, when I began to think I had no other choice: if I wanted to work in India, I might actually have to pay this bribe, even though the thought of it made me sick. At that precise moment, an incredible thing happened.

It was January 30, 1998—the fiftieth anniversary of the death of Mahatma Gandhi. In India, the time of Gandhi's death is observed annually with a moment of complete silence. Television stations go dark, radio programs go quiet, and people everywhere stop what they're doing to stand or sit quietly, remembering.

Inside the auto-rickshaw, at exactly the moment I was thinking, "I might have to pay this bribe," all the traffic around us suddenly screeched to a halt. People got out of their cars, stepped out of shops, and stood utterly still on the sidewalks. "What's happening?" I asked, having forgotten, amid the day's frustration, about the commemoration. As we stepped out of our auto-rickshaw, the driver told me it was the Gandhi death moment.

If this were a scene in a movie, you wouldn't believe it. We had stopped just within view of Hyderabad's massive statue of Gandhi, near the State Assembly. I looked at the great man, sitting cross-legged with his eyes closed, his bald head gleaming in the sun. He looked like he was carrying the weight of the world on his thin shoulders. And at that moment, I thought, *I will never pay this bribe, or any bribe.*

The timing of this moment was nothing short of bizarre, but it jolted me into remembering what was truly important. I didn't offer the bribe, and continued holding out for permission. And instead of sitting idly at my aunt and uncle's house and fretting about the delay, I decided to start working on how SKS would be set up, because I knew now that it might be months before permission came through.

I went to the district census bureau for statistics on poverty in nearby villages, and began studying where we might start our lending. I borrowed money from relatives and rented jeeps so I could go into rural areas and start visiting villages. I began thinking about how to find good loan officers when the money finally did come through. Yet although I was keeping myself busy with important groundwork, I was frustrated beyond measure as the months rolled by and the official still refused permission to bring in my $52,000.

Finally, by the beginning of the Indian summer in April, I'd had enough. I began drafting an editorial for *The Hindu* newspaper, to shine a light on how corruption in India was driving me away. I didn't keep a copy of that essay, but the gist was this: everyone complains that smart, ambitious Indians are leaving the country in droves. Well,

I'm an Indian-American who wanted to come back and do something good for the country, but the government won't let me. So, fine! I'll pack my bags and take my money home to America, and do something there instead.

Biksham and I were still in touch, and I told him my plan. I really was prepared to leave, but not before telling everyone in India what their culture of corruption had wrought. He listened patiently as I ranted, and then, as he always did, he made no pronouncement one way or the other. This was Biksham's way: even when I was working for him at DDS, he almost never gave advice or guidance. He simply listened, then went about his own business.

Which was why I was surprised when, very shortly after that, the permission was granted—thanks to Biksham's intervention. I hadn't asked him to do it, but after we spoke he had made a call over the official's head—to the secretary of the home ministry, the highest ranking official in the ministry—and essentially said, "This kid wants to do something good. You should let him do it." And with that, the months of agonizing were over. It would take a few more months for the money transfer to actually happen, but I was finally free to start SKS. It was the summer of 1998, eight years since I'd first flown to Hyderabad with my gym bag of clothes and dreams of helping Indians. Now it was time to see what I could do. Unfortunately, from the very first step, I found out I had a lot more to learn about India.

CHAPTER FOUR

Rangoli Powder and Handfuls of Seeds

I T WAS A HOT JUNE DAY when I went out into the field with SKS's first employee, a young woman named Rama Laxmi, and suddenly realized just how unprepared I was.

I had hired Rama, a passionate community organizer, after placing an ad in a Hyderabad newspaper, and she was the perfect first employee. She had experience in microfinance and development, she had worked in rural villages, and she was unflappable. This last trait was probably the most important, as she met my

69

bumbling start-up mistakes—and there would be many—with equanimity and poise.

We drove out to the countryside, ready to start recruiting SKS's first members in the villages I'd identified through my census research. Once we'd gotten hundreds of miles outside Hyderabad, I had a flash of realization: there are no hotels out here, in the middle of nowhere! Rama and I had no place to stay, and it was too far to drive back to Hyderabad every night—we'd be on the road for eight hours a day, a colossal waste of precious time.

What to do? I was winging it, as usual, but of course that wouldn't do now that I was traveling with a colleague—an unmarried woman, no less. We began asking around, and I was relieved when a man in one of the towns told us he could help us out with a place to stay. But his solution turned out to be anything but conventional.

"I run a satellite TV business," he told us. "You can sleep at the building where I keep my dish."

As we soon found out, his "satellite TV business" consisted of splicing wires to provide illegal TV service to customers—a common practice in rural India. And the room he was offering us was part of the business. "You have your choice," he said. "You can stay in this room, where we keep the TV on all night to make sure the signal isn't disrupted. Or, if you want, you can sleep on the roof."

We didn't want our sleep disturbed by endless all-night Bollywood movies, so we chose the roof. When I look back now, I can't believe I asked Rama to do this—sleeping on the roof of a random building in her first week of work. To my immense relief and her great credit, she didn't question it at all.

Rama and I stayed on the roof of the satellite building for three nights, until we finally found a room we could rent in a small building nearby. We divided that single room into three parts: my sleeping area, Rama's sleeping area, and our office area. From the standpoint of cultural taboos in conservative rural India, this wasn't much better—but at least we now had a roof over our heads.

With our housing and office needs taken care of—after a fashion, anyway—we set about signing up our first SKS members. We enlisted the help of a couple of stringers for local newspapers, part-time journalists who knew the area very well, and asked them which villages were the poorest, where people would be most in need of loans. We then asked them to come along with us to those villages, to help make introductions.

Rama and I would walk into a village with a stringer, and within a few minutes, the locals started approaching us. Who were we? What did we want? The stringer explained to them that we were starting a new lending program and wanted to meet with them. And soon enough, a group of interested villagers gathered around, ready to hear what we had to say.

When a big enough group had gathered, Rama would ask someone to draw a map of the village, using *rangoli* powder we'd brought. Rangoli powder, similar to chalk powder, is traditionally used for drawing decorative designs on the ground in front of villagers' houses. This was considered a woman's task, so right from the start, we were engaging with local women, one of whom would pick up the powder and start drawing the village.

Once she started drawing, we asked for the basics: Where's the village well? Where does the bus come? Where are the agricultural fields? As the watching crowd grew bigger, we asked more questions: How many small home-front convenience stores—called *kirana* stores— were there? How many tea stalls? Then we'd move into specifics about the villagers themselves. Which households were the poorest? Who needed work?

We also asked the women to diagram the seasonal cash flow. What time of year did the agricultural work pick up? How many days would people typically get work? Were they paid in cash, or in kind? And if in cash, how much? In this way, we could quickly get an idea of how many people in a given village might be receptive to taking a loan, how much they would need, and when.

The techniques we were using were known as participatory rural appraisal, which involved using highly visual group exercises to get villagers to talk about social and economic matters. I had learned and used these techniques during my days at the NGO, DDS, and I had picked up the philosophy behind participatory appraisal through my readings of Robert Chambers.

Normally, villagers would hesitate to answer such direct questions. This would be especially true if we wrote down their answers in notebooks, as most villagers were illiterate, making them suspicious of whatever we might be recording. But by using the rangoli powder, we invited the villagers to actually take part in our mapping. They could see and understand what we were recording, and they even got caught up in the fun of it. In this way, we were able to get a true picture of village life, and we were learning from the best possible source—the villagers themselves. This allowed us to design loan and savings products and create a repayment schedule that would truly meet their needs.

The next step was to launch operations by inviting everyone to come back on an appointed evening for a public village meeting or, as we called it, a projection meeting. In every village, there's the equivalent of a town crier—a man who walks down the dirt roads and paths, banging on a drum and announcing events and news. We'd pay the town crier to announce our meeting, calling on people to meet in the village square. And when we got there, we were usually met by a hundred or so people.

We'd open the projection meeting with a role-play exercise, acting out scenarios explaining the need for microloans and how they work. By play-acting real scenarios—The moneylenders charge too much! The banks are too far away!—we showed how loans from SKS were the cheapest and most reliable option. And at the end of the meeting, we'd invite the women to form themselves into groups of five, so we could start the training program for interested potential borrowers the next day.

We decided on groups of five because that was the basic building block of Grameen's loan program, which we were emulating. Five-member groups were small enough to enforce peer pressure if a member didn't make her payment, and large enough to easily cover a missed repayment if need be. The only other stipulations were that members had to be poor, they couldn't be closely related, they had to live near one another, and they needed to trust each other. Once the women formed themselves into groups, we'd invite them to undergo a seven-day (which we subsequently streamlined to a four-day) training program, both to explain how the loan system worked and to build their trust in each other.

The village women weren't stupid, but they were illiterate, so we needed to explain the concepts of principal, interest, and credit in a way they could understand and remember. We hit on the idea of using currency notes, coins, and small stones to illustrate these concepts visually. On day one of the program, we explained the concept of interest: if you get a two thousand-rupee loan, your weekly installment will be fifty-five rupees. Eight rupees of that is your interest payment, seven goes into your savings, and the rest is paying off the loan principal.

We used small stones to explain how the five-woman groups would work—that if one borrower didn't pay her weekly installment, the other four would have to repay on her behalf. And if those four didn't repay, then the entire village center—as many as forty women—would suffer, with no new loans going out until every payment was made.

This was the essence of the group lending idea pioneered by Grameen Bank. One of the main reasons regular banks won't lend to the poor is that they have no collateral, so the loan would be unsecured. Given that these are illiterate or semiliterate borrowers, and given how small the loan sizes are, conventional banks simply don't think it's worth the risk or the high cost of appraising the loan. By having a group guarantee, we were able to overcome that problem: each group takes responsibility for any missed installment, and if the group isn't able to repay, the entire center is responsible.

In new areas, some villagers didn't believe we would be firm on this rule. After all, the poor were used to seeing the government and NGOs simply waive loans if they didn't repay. So we structured our center meetings such that repayments would come first, then new loans would be disbursed.

Because we staggered the disbursement of loans, rather than giving them out to all members at once, there was strong incentive for whoever was supposed to receive a loan in a given week to make sure all repayments were made. Otherwise they wouldn't receive their loan. Weekly meetings were supposed to last an hour or so, but in the beginning they went a little longer, because if one borrower failed to make a payment, we would refuse to disburse new loans until the others managed to cobble together her share.

Often, when we started lending in a new village and no one happened to be waiting for a loan on a particular week, people decided to test us by willfully not paying. But we instructed our loan officers not to leave the meeting until the repayment came in. In some cases, a loan officer would have to wait for hours, occasionally even into the evening. If he had another meeting to attend, he would call the branch office for a replacement person. Or, if no one was available, he would leave his collected cash and papers there and go to his next meeting. The borrowers would end up waiting, since it was not ethically accepted to walk out if the meeting had not closed and the cash was lying there. This had a powerful social effect. The entire village would realize there was some issue, and they'd learn that everyone was waiting in the meeting because someone didn't repay. And that person would lose *izzath*—lose face. Losing face is a fairly devastating thing in a village context, and people will do anything to avoid it. So as long as we showed our firmness from the start, we typically never had a repayment standoff again.

This is not to say that we insisted on a borrower's repaying even if she was facing a hardship. Instead, we wanted to convey that while being a member gave you the benefit of receiving loans, one of the duties of being a member was to help others out in times of difficulty. We inculcated this sense of responsibility through a cooperation game, a technique that Rama had used in an earlier development job and then adapted for SKS.

We created a little cardboard hut for each woman and divided it into five pieces, like a jigsaw puzzle. Then, we mixed all the pieces from all the huts together, and gave each woman five random pieces. The task was for them to rebuild their little five-piece huts—without talking to each other.

The women made eye contact and passed their pieces around, helping each other and trying out combinations until everyone's hut was rebuilt correctly. "This is how group lending works," Rama told them. "You can't do it on your own. You have to help each other out." We continued to hone and refine the approach over time, but these basic tools would continue to serve us very well.

The second employee I hired was an idealistic young village woman named Nirmala Kambalimatam. Fresh out of high school, Nirmala brought something neither Rama nor I had: a local perspective. Because she'd grown up in a village, she had a much deeper understanding of village life and codes. Even simply hiring her was educational for me—I had to ask her parents for permission to hire her at SKS, and she initially told them that she was working at a bank so they wouldn't object.

Rama and I were outsiders in this rural world, and we were apt to make mistakes without even knowing it, so Nirmala was our guide. Once, for example, Rama and I started bringing fake cash to villages, to show how loans and interest work. I thought this approach was pretty clever, until Nirmala told us there was a counterfeiting ring known to be operating in the area. What kind of charlatans would waltz into a village with obviously fake cash? Not the best way to build trust, clearly.

The days were long and intense. Poor people are generally available early in the morning, as they often work in the fields during the day, so we would get up before dawn and have our first village meetings at 7 a.m. Then Rama, Nirmala, and I would come back to our little office and meet, to talk about what worked and what didn't. We were working from Grameen Bank replication manuals, but they were incomplete and in some cases unhelpful, so we were constantly making changes.

In the daytime, when villagers were unavailable, we spent hours meeting with government people, gathering information, and taking care of accounts and loan documentation. And in the evenings, we'd conduct group trainings and projection meetings in new villages. We usually didn't finish until 11 p.m., making the days incredibly long and draining.

It was all worth it, though, on the day we handed out our very first loan. Our first member was an older woman named Sathamma who wanted the loan to start a vegetable vending business. She was a colorful character in her village—a woman who'd seen it all and wasn't afraid to speak her mind. "I'm not taking more than a thousand rupees," she snapped when we discussed her first loan. "I can only handle a thousand. So don't try to make me take more, and don't give me a hard time!" Laughing, I promised we wouldn't.

As it turned out, my father was in India the week we were finally ready to start disbursing loans. I invited him to come to the village for the first loan, on June 28, 1998, and he drove out from Hyderabad to join us in the borrowers' circle. When the moment came, I asked my father to hand the cash to Sathamma. I hadn't really planned it, but it seemed the right thing to do, having our first loan come directly from my father's hand. At long last, after all the preparation, sweat, and headaches, SKS was in business.

It was a thrilling moment. But the headaches weren't over yet—not by a long shot.

THE RURAL AREA WHERE we launched SKS operations, Narayankhed, is described locally as *kathernak*, a word that translates roughly to "dangerous and nasty place." It's the backwater of all backwaters, a neglected, desolate, and poverty-stricken region where the hardships of life are etched in people's faces. Narayankhed is so unwelcoming that social workers, government employees, and others who are posted there are usually considered to be receiving a "punishment" posting.

I picked this region partly because it was so desperate, and partly because it was just a three-hour bus drive from the DDS compound, which meant that many villagers had at least heard of DDS. Being able to tell villagers I had worked for an organization they'd heard of brought us one step closer to establishing trust. And anything we could do to establish and maintain trust was critical, because without it we'd be doomed from the start.

But trust could be elusive, as we soon discovered.

In our first village, the second loan we gave out was for a woman to buy a goat. This was a popular and easy way for villagers to make money: you could buy a goat and take it along with you to the agricultural fields, where it would graze while you worked, as a goat will eat just about anything. You could then breed the goat and sell its kids when you needed money.

In this case, we knew the borrower already had one goat, but she wanted to increase her business. The week after we gave the woman her loan, we came back to check on whether she'd actually bought a new goat. This was another principle I learned from Grameen: it was good to check on borrowers to make sure they were using loans for their stated purpose. Otherwise, the money would too often end up going for household expenses or other, non-income-generating purchases.

Rama and I drove to the village, and we met the woman at her house. "I bought the goat!" she said brightly. "Here it is!" With a flourish, she gestured to a skinny brown goat standing nearby.

"Great," I said, and smiled at the woman.

"Wait!" said Rama. "This is not a new goat. This is the one we saw last week. It's the same color, with the same markings." I looked at Rama, amazed. How many goats had we seen, in how many villages? And she remembered that this goat was the same one she'd seen a week ago? How could she tell?

"No, it's not the old goat!" the woman protested. "I just bought it! The one you saw last week was black."

But Rama stood firm. "We're not stupid," she told the woman. "This is the same goat we saw last week."

It felt absurd to be standing in a dusty village in the middle of nowhere, arguing with a woman over the color of a goat. Was this what I'd spent all these years preparing to do? But we knew we had to make it absolutely clear, from the very beginning, that we wouldn't bend the rules for anyone. If SKS was going to establish not only trust, but also a culture of accountability, we had to be firm.

Rama wouldn't back down, and the woman finally confessed. Yes, she admitted, this was the old goat. She really wanted the loan, but she intended to use it to buy food. "You can't use it for that," Rama told her. "Buying food doesn't generate any income, so you'll be no closer to getting out of poverty that way. Either buy a new goat, or give us back the loan money." The woman eventually agreed, and the next week when we checked in again, she had bought a new goat.

That situation ended well, but others did not. Sometimes, being firm with destitute, even desperate, people felt cruel rather than strategic. This was especially true when one person's carelessness resulted in hardship for another.

In one incident, a woman had made a partial deposit to lease a piece of land. She wanted to start an agricultural business, and she planned to use her SKS loan to pay the remainder of the deposit. Unfortunately, another woman in the group came late to the meeting—and our rules were clear: no one in a group could receive a loan if any member was late to that week's meeting.

"I'm sorry," I said to the woman. "But we can't give you your loan. You know the rules."

"But I'll lose my deposit!" she said, her voice rising. "It's not my fault she came late!" Other women in the group nodded their heads—it didn't seem fair! But we had to stay firm, no matter how sick it made me feel in the pit of my stomach. For years, villagers had received subsidized credit from government programs and simply failed to pay back their loans. There was a culture of bad credit that the government couldn't—or wouldn't—do anything about, but if we fell into that same pattern, SKS wouldn't survive. So we had to be absolutely strict and consistent, even when it was painful to see.

We didn't give her the loan that week, but she devised a way to buy more time. In rural India, chicken is a precious commodity. She prepared a chicken dinner for the man she owed the money to, and asked him to give her one more week to pay him. He agreed, and the next week, everyone showed up at the meeting promptly. She got her loan, and her fellow borrowers got to see firsthand how important it was to support the group as a whole. We never had a problem with attendance or on-time repayment in that village again.

Even harder were situations when someone's luck simply turned bad. One borrower used her loan to purchase a plow bull—a surefire moneymaker in agricultural areas, and an investment that should have paid off for years to come. Unfortunately, just two weeks after the woman bought her bull, it up and died. Our policy in such cases was to waive the interest on her loan, but she still had to pay back the principal, week after week, with no means of making that extra money. It was heart-wrenching.

There was a good reason we couldn't waive repayment of loans for animals that later died: livestock fraud is a burgeoning industry in rural India. Sometimes villagers would kill their goats to eat the meat, then try to make a claim for the dead animal. Other people even would cut off the ear of an animal and present it as proof it had died—then sell the one-eared animal to someone else. There just was no foolproof way to know if someone was telling the truth when they claimed an animal had died.

We took an equally firm approach to the rules of our seven-day training in each new village. If someone did not show up on time, we'd just pack up and leave. The late-comer would get an earful for inconveniencing the whole group, and invariably everyone would be on time the next day. From the very beginning, I knew that SKS could succeed only if we kept the trains running on time. Village life runs on a different schedule, and unless we insisted on punctuality, people would come late, meetings would drag on too long, and we'd have trouble serving all the villages we needed to in a given day.

We applied that same level of discipline to our field staff, many of whom were the first in their family to be educated, through affirmative action programs, and some of whom were working their first job ever. Unfortunately, some of them—especially those who'd worked somewhere else first—came to us with bad habits, such as showing up late.

So, to establish immediately that this wouldn't be tolerated, we adhered to deadlines and sent back potential recruits—even if they came from far away—if they were late. Likewise, we had strict cutoffs for recruitment tests, and even missing the cutoff by a single point meant that the candidate wouldn't get picked. This was a painful to enforce, especially since some of our early candidates were sons and daughters of our newest members, or in some cases children of villagers I had worked with at DDS. But we had to do it.

We also continued the same firm approach after a recruit joined SKS, especially when it came to money matters. In one case, a former field colleague of mine from DDS had "borrowed" from his training kit the handful of coins and currency notes we used to train borrowers—about 3oo rupees, or $6. When we did a random check and found the money missing, I fired him on the spot. This might seem a Draconian response, but we had to be a good steward of people's money—whether it belonged to our funders or our poor members.

As SKS grew, we hired more loan officers and expanded into more villages. Because cell phones weren't as prevalent in rural India in the late '9os, most of our employees didn't have them—so the only way to know a loan officer was having trouble collecting repayments was if he or she didn't come back to the branch office at the usual time. Whenever that happened, another loan officer would hop on a moped and head out to the village to find out what had happened, and relieve the first loan officer if needed.

We also encountered problems when our female loan officers began riding mopeds—the cheap and versatile transport of choice in rural India—to the villages. Mopeds had long been a popular way for Indian men to get around. But women didn't drive them, especially in conservative rural areas. If they rode them at all, they rode sidesaddle, behind a male driver. It had always been that way.

So when our female loan officers started driving mopeds around, the reaction was swift and unequivocal. Men didn't like it, and they let the women know. Some of our employees were teased, but others experienced more serious harassment, even threats.

The first time Nirmala was scheduled to go alone to an evening meeting, I was concerned enough about her safety that I asked one of our male employees to surreptitiously follow her to the village. I didn't want Nirmala to know, as it might damage her self-confidence to know I was sending a "minder" to watch over her. I also wanted to hear from the male employee how bad the harassment was. "Stay behind her," I told him, "but not close enough anyone can tell you're following her."

That evening, as I heard Nirmala's moped putter back to the branch office, I was anxious to hear how things had gone. I had never seen Nirmala flustered, but she came running into the office with a look of terror on her face.

"Someone was following me!" she said, breathless with fear. "Every time I looked back, he was there!"

Oops. Not my most brilliant executive moment. I had to confess that I'd secretly sent someone to follow her. So much for my attempts to protect my employees! I ended up terrorizing Nirmala more than anyone else ever had.

M EANWHILE, BACK IN THE United States, a tech revolution was taking place. While I was living in primitive conditions in rural India, on the other side of the world Silicon Valley was aflame with creativity, entrepreneurialism—and money. The Internet boom was in full swing, and venture capitalists were funding start-ups left and right. Not only was the boom changing the way the world communicated, it was also making a lot of young millionaires, many of whom happened to be Indian.

One of those newly minted millionaires was named Ravi Reddy. Ravi and his business partner Sandeep Tungare had cofounded a company called Think Systems, which created demand-management software for companies like Nabisco and Dell. Ravi was in the right place at the right time with the right product, and in mid-1997, when he and Sandeep closed the sale of their company to i2 Technologies for $150 million, he was suddenly in a position to give money to causes he cared about.

I had known Ravi a long time—we're actually distantly related—and had hit him up for an initial donation in early 1997. At that point, he was interested in SKS, but he was working 24/7 on Think Systems and was not in a position to do anything substantial. On one of my trips back to the States, I heard he'd sold his company, but didn't know the details. Then my mom told me he'd invited me to come by and visit while I was home.

I stopped by to see him, expecting little more than a friendly chat. But I got my first clue that things with Ravi were very different now the moment I pulled up to his house. Before, he'd lived in a modest home in a nice neighborhood. When I arrived at the address he'd given me, I parked in front of a mansion.

Ravi greeted me warmly, then got right to business. He told me he and Sandeep wanted to put some of their money to work in India, but they didn't particularly like the NGO model. We talked about my belief that aggressively for-profit microfinance would allow for faster, broader, more sustainable growth than nonprofits. He knew I was planning to turn SKS into a for-profit company as soon as we were able, and he liked the notion of putting money into an entrepreneurial venture.

"I've been following your progress, Vikram," he told me. "We want to make a donation of $50,000."

I was stunned. Our entire budget for the first year of operations was the original $52,000 I had raised. My salary was being paid by a two-year grant from the Echoing Green Foundation, at $30,000 per year. With those two sources of money we had just scraped enough together to survive—but now, with this one check, Ravi and Sandeep were doubling our budget for operations. That initial funding—plus Ravi's ongoing financial support and business guidance over the years—would prove absolutely critical to our eventual success.

Ravi and Sandeep's vote of confidence made it easier to face the continuing hardships of starting up the business back in India. In those early days, our biggest problem was countering the lies of the local moneylenders. Before SKS—or Basix, or Cashpor, or any other reputable microfinance provider—came on the scene, these moneylenders were often the only source of loans for villagers.

Local moneylenders charged exorbitant rates for their loans, usually 4 percent a month, but sometimes as much as 10 percent, which works out to an annual percentage rate of 48 to 120 percent. At such rates, anyone who fell behind on a payment could never expect to catch up—even just a couple of months in, your interest burden would already be so high that you'd simply enter an endless debt spiral. In some cases, moneylenders would demand that a male member of the household become "bonded labor," meaning he had to work for the moneylender at a low price to pay off the debt. In this way, moneylenders were able to solidify control in their villages.

At SKS, we started out charging 36 percent interest, which sounds incredibly high when compared to Western loan rates of 10 to 12 percent. But there was no other option, given the very different circumstances surrounding loans to the poor. First, the cost of servicing these loans was much higher: in the West, your banker doesn't come to you each week to collect your loan payment face-to-face. But SKS loan officers traveled to every village, every week, to sit with the women and collect their payments.

Second, because the average size of our loans was so small, it wasn't financially feasible to charge, say, 10 percent interest—those tiny repayments wouldn't even cover the cost of fuel for getting the loan officer to the villages. Finally, all the loans we were disbursing were handed out with no collateral whatsoever. We were going out on a limb, trying to be financially viable, and we had to have a small cushion in case borrowers didn't repay their loans. And while it may sound strange to Western ears, even at 36 percent interest the poor were able to run microbusinesses that enabled them to pay off their loans and still have a large surplus—our borrowers averaged about a 50 percent profit margin.

The truth is, we actually could have charged much higher interest rates than we did, while still significantly undercutting the moneylenders. But our goal was not to be extractive; it was to make enough profit to cover our costs and fund further growth. And funding growth was expensive: we had to rent branch office space, recruit and train new staff, equip them with mopeds, buy computers and supplies, and so on. So, even charging 36 percent interest, we ran a deficit for several years before breaking even. But eventually, thanks to a greater volume of members and improved efficiency, we did break even and when that happened, we dropped our interest rates from 36 percent to 30 percent to 28 percent, where they stand now. Whenever we first approached a village about offering loans, there were numerous reasons why villagers preferred to borrow from us. Not only did we offer lower interest rates than the moneylenders, we also didn't respond with violence when repayments weren't made, and we fostered a general sense of group support rather than leaving borrowers to struggle on their own. For all these reasons, moneylenders hated to see us come to town. We were stealing their business.

So they fought back, in a number of ways. First would be rumors: they'd tell villagers that SKS was from America, and that we were really a front for a Christian evangelical group. Villagers would hear that we aimed to get them into debt, then forcibly convert them. Christian evangelists had been trickling into India for generations, but in recent years they had become more numerous, and more active. Tagging SKS with that identity was an easy way to turn villagers away from us.

If that didn't work, other rumors soon followed. When male loan officers went into new villages, moneylenders would whisper, "Who's this guy, coming to your villages and asking for young women?" Stories circulated that we were trapping women into prostitution, or even that I had come back from America to steal money from Indians. And when our female loan officers went into new towns, they often heard veiled threats along the lines of, "You know this is very dangerous work for a woman, don't you?"

For these reasons, we tended to look for people to introduce us in each village. If we met someone who lived in a village where we weren't yet offering loans, we'd ask them to take us there and introduce us around. Unfortunately, this didn't always work out as planned.

On one memorable occasion, a young woman walked into a branch office to ask about our loans. She was from a village where we'd tried, and failed, to find an "in," so I was particularly excited she had shown up. She was young, progressive, and articulate—I couldn't believe our luck!

I went with her to the village, and we started walking around and chatting. This had become our usual way of launching in a new village—just strolling around, starting conversations and gauging interest. People in the village seemed intrigued, so we asked the town crier to call for a projection meeting the following evening.

Yet when we arrived the next evening at the appointed time, no one was there. Not a single person had showed up, but a few were hovering around the edges, seemingly curious as to whether anyone else would come. What was going on? Usually we got at least a hundred people at these projection meetings. Everything had gone so well the day before, yet now we were getting the cold shoulder. We waited about a half-hour, then returned to the branch office, disappointed and confused.

As we learned later, the woman who had introduced us to the village was well known. A little too well known, in fact—she was the local prostitute. I felt ridiculous—here I'd been wandering around this town with her, saying, "Join our group! Come on and join our group!" No wonder we'd gotten the cold shoulder. To this day I don't know whether the woman had come to us genuinely seeking a loan, or whether she was simply seeking a new client for herself.

Even in the "Wild West" atmosphere of those first two years, there were only a few times when I felt truly, physically threatened. For the most part, the interference we got from moneylenders and meddlesome, bribe-seeking bureaucrats was more of a nuisance than anything else. But on a couple of occasions, I wondered whether I too was going to be on the receiving end of an assault.

The first incident came after we repeatedly turned down a local politician who kept trying to extort us. He'd come to us and say, "I want you to hire these three people for SKS. They don't need to work, just put them on your payroll." Or, "I need to borrow one of your jeeps tomorrow. Make sure it's at my house." I kept saying no to everything, but still the requests kept coming.

Finally, he got tired of hearing "no." So he called me to his office for a little talk.

"New people who come to our region need to cooperate with local ways," he told me. He was absolutely calm, not thuggish or overtly threatening. He spoke with sophistication, but his message was primitive and clear. "Remember," he told me, "in Narayankhed, sometimes murders can even happen for such things."

I was scared and upset to have been so obviously threatened. Would this local politician really resort to violence? I had no way of knowing, and didn't want to find out. I called a few of my relatives in Hyderabad, including one uncle who was well connected in this area. "What should I do?" I asked him. "I don't know how to handle this."

My uncle arranged a meeting for me with the chief minister of Andhra Pradesh, a much higher-level politician than the man who had threatened me. It was set up as simply an informational meeting, where I could tell the chief minister about SKS and our work—in fact, during our conversation, I never mentioned the local politician. But word spread that I had enough connections to have met with the chief minister, and that was enough to get the other politician to back off. He knew this was a signal to him that I had a higher level of protection, so I never heard another request from him.

This was the way I preferred to deal with most problems: I wanted to make them go away in the simplest, most direct way possible. All I cared about was the work, and anything that impeded it had to be taken care of. Unfortunately, as the next incident showed, it wasn't always so easy to take care of such things.

.   .   .

A T THE END OF 1998, six months after disbursing our first loan, we had 165 borrowers. We were operating in eight villages and had seven staff members—all loan officers. We had one branch office, where we took care of accounts and payroll matters, and we had expanded beyond that initial room that Rama and I had shared, taking more rooms on the same floor of that same building.

By mid-1999, we had grown to about ten employees, and managing them all, plus developing and sustaining the business, was becoming too big a task for me. So I hired my first executive: a polished, English-speaking, highly qualified chief operations officer. His name was Shyam Mohan.

We had recently purchased some land outside one of the villages, where we planned to build a DDS-style compound. This would be our first branch office, and eventually I envisioned having a kind of rural headquarters. Two small buildings sat on our plot of land, and the plan was to use one as living quarters and the other as an office.

I wanted to show Shyam the site, so he, his wife, and I went there one night after wrapping up work in Hyderabad for the day. By the time we got there, it was late—maybe one or two o'clock in the morning, so our plan was to spend the night and look around in the morning. We parked and walked up to the door of one building, and the first thing I noticed was that the electricity was off.

Now, this was not an unusual occurrence in rural India. Electricity was, and still is, an unpredictable luxury rather than a given. I assumed it was a typical temporary power failure and didn't think any more about it. Shyam and his wife went into the room they'd be sharing, and I went into mine, right next to it. We said goodnight, and shut our doors.

A couple of hours later, in the absolute dead of night, I was awakened by the clacking of someone locking my door from the outside. I jumped out of bed and rushed to push the door open, but it wouldn't budge. I was trapped in my room!

I started yelling just as I heard the pounding on Shyam's door. I looked out the window, and though it was pitch black, I could make out the forms of five or six men, some of whom were carrying crowbars. They were beating on Shyam's door. I could hear Shyam yelling, too—both of us were screaming at the top of our lungs, trying to get some-one's attention before these men broke Shyam's door down and did who knows what.

These men were on the attack: they pounded savagely at Shyam's door, whacking it with their crowbars. I felt com-pletely helpless, trapped in my little room while a gang of thugs was threatening my COO and his wife. Even if I could get out of the room, what could I do? There were six of them and one of me, and they were armed. So I just yelled and yelled, desperately hoping someone from the nearby village would hear and come save us.

The men pounded on Shyam's door for what felt like an hour, before finally giving up and leaving as quickly as they'd come. When it seemed the danger had passed, Shyam and his wife opened their door, unlocked mine, and we stayed together in my room. We stayed awake the rest of the night, holding makeshift weapons in case the thugs returned. Shyam and his wife were, not surprisingly, completely terrorized.

To this day, I don't know who was behind the attack. It might have been ordered by a local moneylender who didn't like what SKS was doing. It might have been an intimidation tactic from a local politician. The one thing we did learn was that the power outage was anything but routine: someone had cut the electrical wires to the buildings. The attack was premeditated, and it worked. The next morning a traumatized Shyam told me, "I can't do this, Vikram. I quit."

I had certainly been afraid the night before, but deep down I never really believed anything truly terrible could happen to us. Would thugs really attack and beat an American for working in their village? Wouldn't that just cause more trouble than it was worth for them? I still don't know what those attackers' ultimate goal was, but I suspect it was to frighten us away from the work we were doing. Instead it just left me more determined to press on.

Yet now we faced a bigger and more enduring problem than random thugs trying to scare us away: how could we ramp up operations quickly and efficiently, to serve even more poor Indians? This was the problem that had bedeviled microfinance providers for decades, and it was the problem I hoped to solve. Now came the true test—could it be done? And how?

CHAPTER FIVE

The McDonald's of Microfinance

B Y THE END of our second full fiscal year, in April of 2000, SKS was serving 695 members and had disbursed about $25,000 in loans. We'd started slowly because we had to—but now it was time to begin ramping up our numbers. If the first two years were about creating a solid, stable base for operations, the next two would be about streamlining our systems and increasing our growth rate. We were off to the races.

Unfortunately, as I soon discovered, it was still hard to get others in the field to take us seriously. In 2000, I went to a dinner in Seattle hosted by the Grameen Foundation USA. The foundation had decided to focus on the three largest MFIs in India: Cashpor, Share, and ASA. I had managed to finagle an invitation, but SKS was still the skinny kid on the playground, waiting to be picked.

I ended up in a conversation with Steve Rockefeller, a grandson of Nelson Rockefeller who was an executive at Deutsche Bank and a Grameen Foundation USA board member. We talked about SKS, and I told him about our plans for expansion. Either I didn't explain it well or he didn't quite believe me, because in response he said, "Maybe you could become a franchisee of one of these other MFIs."

He meant well, no doubt. But I had no intention of becoming a franchisee of anyone, and I found the notion vaguely insulting. I'll admit that I have an ego, and this comment definitely provoked it. I now realized that the only way to convince people we were serious about our business model—about growing faster and serving more poor people than any MFI in history—was to just knuckle down and do it. No one had ever come close to growing at the pace I envisioned for us, and no one seemed to believe it was possible. But I believed I could find a way.

It started with a bottle of Coca-Cola. One dust-choked afternoon in rural India, I bought a Coke at a roadside stand. As I gratefully gulped it down, I found myself thinking: how did that company manage to scale globally at such a rapid pace? A few years earlier, you couldn't buy a Coke anywhere in India—the company ceased operations between 1977 and 1993 due to a fight with the Indian government over revealing its secret formula.

But in 1993, the Coca-Cola Company returned to India and expanded at a breathtaking pace, and soon you could find that familiar red logo in the remotest corners of the country. The same was true of other aggressive companies, like Starbucks and McDonald's—when they decided to expand, they were instantly everywhere. How did they do it? And what lessons could we take from them to help SKS do the same?

All of a sudden, it came to me. A Coke is a Coke is a Coke, no matter where you buy it. It's a single, standardized product that is made, shipped, and sold in the same way everywhere. Coke was able to scale so rapidly because it had a very simple product in a recognizable, standardized package. Why couldn't we create similar products, loan and insurance products for the poor that were standardized across the board, no matter where we offered them, and to whom?

The answer was, we could. And so we did.

We had already taken the first step, by offering loans only in preset amounts. We realized from the start that if we offered different loan amounts for different borrowers, we'd end up with a confusing jumble of numbers for the loan officers. And because we were tracking all of our numbers by hand, the potential for mistakes was just too high. If a loan officer has five hundred borrowers, each of whom has a weekly loan repayment as well as an insurance payment, that loan officer will be making more than 150,000 individual entries per year—on cardboard passbooks, paper collection sheets, and thick dusty branch ledgers—all by hand. But with standardized amounts and an unchanging interest rate, the loan officers would have to note only variations, not every individual entry. That was the first step.

The next step was to eliminate coins. We set the loan repayments at round numbers, so loan officers wouldn't have to count and carry coins, a simple enough fix that made their work that much easier. We also required borrowers to hand over their weekly payments with the bills flattened, stacked face up, and divided into denominations, so the loan officer could count them quickly. Before, they'd bring bills that had been crumpled and stuffed into the folds of saris, and the loan officers had to smooth the bills out before they could even begin to count them.

These sound like obvious, minor fixes—but they made a tremendous difference in time. Before I launched SKS, I'd watched a number of meetings run by other MFIs; invariably, their loan officers spent large amounts of time counting coins and painstakingly recording differing numbers in passbooks. These simple changes helped our loan officers shave significant time off their meetings, which in turn allowed them to schedule more meetings per day, further cutting our administrative and staff costs.

I became obsessed with the idea of cutting meeting times down to the absolute minimum required. My model for this was McDonald's: at any McDonald's in the world, a customer can walk in and get food served within minutes. I had even seen little timers by the cashiers showing "average time to serve," with forty-five to sixty seconds being a typical average. The transactions at our borrowers' meetings were certainly no more complex than those at McDonald's, so why couldn't our loan officers function just as quickly?

I began taking a stopwatch out to the villages, to time our loan officers in action. We looked at every possible place to shave even a couple of minutes off the meetings, and over time they became tighter and tighter. Today, if you were to sit in on an SKS borrowers' meeting, you'd see a completely streamlined, assembly-line-style process, with loan officers and borrowers moving smoothly and quickly through their scheduled tasks. We also make sure each loan officer's daily meetings are scheduled in villages that lie along a single road, so the employee can travel quickly between them. As a result, our loan officers are able to run more meetings per week than those of other MFIs doing comparable, rural-based loan work.

With these improvements in place, we'd now taken care of the second of the three *c*'s: capacity. We knew the problem of capital would be solved when SKS converted into a for-profit entity and we were able to solicit investors. But that couldn't happen until we solved the other *c* problem: cost.

How could we lower the very high transaction costs of offering microloans? Very simply, we needed to cut down on the number of staff hours it took to log and maintain records of our loans. But the only way to do that was by trying something very few other MFIs were doing—something, in fact, that many in the field thought was an expensive folly. We needed to develop an easy, scalable, cheap software system that our loan officers, many of whom had only high school educations and no computer experience, could use.

Ever since I'd seen that Grameen Bank employee hand-copy ten years' worth of a member's loan information, I knew we had to find a way to automate the business of tracking loans. Most MFIs recorded their transactions in three places—borrowers' passbooks, collection sheets, and, finally, back-office ledgers. There was simply no way we could grow at the rate I wanted while recording all these transactions by hand.

So, two years after we launched, I committed about $250,000 to developing an easy-to-use software suite, specially designed for our needs. At the time, our entire loan portfolio was only about $25,000, so this was a huge—some even called it reckless—leap. Grameen Bank and Cashpor had begun working on automated systems at around the same time, and we ended up recruiting a volunteer developer who had done some initial work for them. His name was Bala Krishnamurti.

I knew Bala from Chicago, and he was a brilliant developer who took his job very seriously. He, Rama, and I started working together to figure out exactly what we needed, which right away turned out to be more difficult than expected.

"I need to know what exactly the loan officers do," Bala told us, "so I can design the software to address those needs most efficiently."

I started to answer him, but he interrupted me. "No," he said. "Let me hear it from a front-line loan officer."

Bala and I traveled to one of our branches to talk to Nirmala, our first loan officer. As she began to describe the process to Bala, I was surprised—she was already doing certain things a little differently than I thought. So much for standardization! If we couldn't keep all our loan officers on the same tasks when we were small, could we really do it when we started growing exponentially? We needed this software more than ever, as having a single software suite that everyone used would help solve that problem.

We needed something easy to use, flexible, and as cheap as possible to develop. Unfortunately, you almost always have to sacrifice one of those factors to get the other two. So Bala, Rama, and I began heated debates about what to sacrifice—or, more correctly, Bala and Rama debated and I played the arbiter. Rama would say, "We must have the ability to set up three different repayment schedules—biweekly, weekly, and monthly!" Bala would pipe back, "But that will significantly increase our costs!" All I could hope was that despite the disagreements, Rama's input from the field and Bala's creativity with software code would lead us to a design for an efficient and cost-effective system.

Once we agreed on the deliverables, Bala recruited two local developers. After twelve months of work our fledgling IT team created a software product that did absolutely everything we needed: it had a simple, logical interface that worked on a point-and-click basis, with language fonts that could be adjusted to match local languages and dialects, and it integrated portfolio tracking with accounts. It was incredibly easy to use, so much so that, as one of our loan officers later told the *Wall Street Journal*, she had two skills: "I know sewing and I know the SKS system."

Because we had standardized the loan repayments, loan officers could prepopulate the blanks in the online forms with those amounts, drastically cutting down on the hours needed to update records. Bala did such an excellent job that we used essentially the same system for nearly a decade—and even when we invested in a $2 million overhaul of the system in 2008, it was only to accommodate more products on the back end of the software. The interface and front end have remained the same.

With that initial investment in software, we had solved the final *c*—cost—and could begin ramping up in earnest. But I wanted to push the technological barrier even further, after an experience I had on another visit back in the United States.

I was living full time in India, so on periodic trips back home I needed to rent a car. One afternoon, while turning in my latest rental before catching a flight back, I noticed that the Hertz attendant used a handheld device right at the car to process my account and print a bill. It was quick and elegant, and far more efficient than having everyone walk into the Hertz office and stand in line. When I returned to India I began telling people about the handheld, and to my surprise our chartered accountant, a man named V. Nagarajan, had come up with the same idea: why couldn't SKS do the same thing?

Would it be possible for our loan officers to use handhelds in the field, rather than logging loan repayments by hand, and then automating them once they got back to the branch office? Even though our new software had improved our efficiency tremendously, we'd be even better off if we could eliminate that first step of hand-copying the repayment amounts.

In 2000, when we first began exploring the use of handhelds, not many companies were using them. A few rental car companies, as well as Federal Express and other package-delivery services, were the only ones I'd seen employing this new technology—and one of the reasons was, it was expensive. Like any new technology, the price would drop after initial adopters starting using it, but these types of handhelds hadn't reached that point yet.

With that in mind, when we started experimenting with handhelds for SKS, I looked for the cheapest hardware I could find. We bought several refurbished Palm Pilots from Overstock.com and designed an application that involved using smart cards that could be inserted in them. So now, rather than having a paper passbook for recording loans and repayments, each borrower would have a smart card—basically an electronic passbook—that could be inserted into the loan officer's Palm Pilot to transfer the information digitally. The loan officer could then transfer all of the group's information directly from the Palm Pilot into the computer at the branch office.

We ran this pilot project for one year, and from a technology perspective it was a great success. But there was one problem: we could only justify a full rollout of the program, with its costly investment in hardware and training, if borrowers could also use the smart cards as cash substitutes.

At the time we launched the Palm/smart card project, regulators, bankers, and payments providers were pushing for the creation of a payment infrastructure—ATMs and points-of-sale—in rural areas. Unfortunately, the regulation to do so never emerged, making it impossible to use the smart cards as cash substitutes. So, even if we rolled out the use of handhelds, our loan officers would still have to deal with two tasks: handling cash payments and inputting amounts. This wasn't efficient enough to justify the cost, so we shelved the program—although, at this writing, we're looking into reviving the project using mobile phones.

Despite the setback of not being able to use smart cards, by 2002 we had our software and our "Coke-ified" standard practices, and we were ready to begin explosive growth. At the end of our fiscal year 2000, we'd had 695 members and had disbursed around $25,000 in loans. At the end of FY 2001, we had 1,922 members and had disbursed $117,243 in loans. Then, the numbers began shooting up: at the end of FY 2002, we had 5,819 members and $543,285 in loans disbursed; and by the end of FY 2003 we had 13,519 members and cumulatively disbursed more than $2.4 million in loans. The expansion plan was working.

Despite all the streamlining and growth, even more unexpected hurdles kept popping up to threaten our work—some that were very personal for me, and others that bordered on the bizarre.

TWO YEARS AFTER founding SKS, I had gotten married to a woman I first met in graduate school. Malini and I had first started dating back in 1996, but we broke up soon afterward, as she knew I planned to move to India, and she wanted to stay in the States. The breakup was amicable, and when we ran into each other again in September of 1999, during an extended visit home, we reconnected. Very quickly, after just a few weeks of dating again, we decided to get married.

The reality was, I had become lonely working in rural Indian villages. The work was exciting, meaningful, and very busy, but it was also isolating. Even though I was around people all day, it was difficult to connect to them on a personal level because our lives were so different. I missed relationships with people who shared my background and were familiar with American culture. Some days I felt like a missionary of sorts, out in the hinterlands doing the most fulfilling work I could imagine—yet feeling very lonely at the same time.

Also, I was living in a very traditional culture, where being unmarried at age twenty-nine was considered odd. The first few times villagers expressed surprise on learning I was single, I didn't mind. But by the hundredth time, it had really started to wear on me. I began to wonder if they were right—if there was something wrong with being unmarried and so focused on my work.

So when Malini and I started dating again, and she indicated that she might reconsider living in India, I was ecstatic. We married in December of 1999, and although I went back to India right afterward, she stayed in the States to finish law school. For the first year or so we had a long-distance marriage, but then, in February of 2001, our son was born. Now I was more anxious than ever for her—and our son—to join me in India. But Malini told me she didn't want to go, that especially with a new baby, she wanted to stay in the comfortable suburbs of Chicago. I was devastated, but there seemed to be no middle ground. Eventually, we could not reconcile our differences, and in October of 2001, we separated.

The marriage had lasted eighteen months, and the divorce, which grew increasingly acrimonious, took almost as long. By December of 2002, when everything was finalized, I was not only emotionally spent, I was financially tapped out from attorneys' fees. And now I had a young son who was living in Chicago with his mother while I was in India full time. I couldn't stand the thought of being away from him so much.

Financially and personally, this was the absolute worst period of my life. SKS was doing great—growing just as I'd hoped and planned. But I was crushed under a $90,000 graduate school debt plus divorce fees, as under Illinois law the primary income earner must pay the attorneys' fees for both spouses. And with our divorce proceedings having gone on for so long, due in part to the fact that Malini was a divorce lawyer and knew how to prolong proceedings, those fees were astronomical—around $100,000.

I'd been earning a minimal NGO salary for my entire working life, averaging about $40,000 a year for my first six years at SKS; there was no way I could even start to dig out from under my mountain of debt, and I had no savings at all. In fact, in order to pay the divorce attorneys' fees, I was forced to borrow from family and run up credit cards—and I was already carrying another $45,000 in personal credit card debt from taking cash advances over the years to help fund SKS deficits.

Eventually, I realized I had no choice: I would have to resign as CEO of SKS to get my life back in order. I informed the board, while telling them I wanted to stay actively involved as chair.

After a transition period, I had a tearful farewell with our staff in India. I couldn't quite believe that my tenure as CEO was ending like this, but I just didn't see any way around it. The sole comforting factor was that by now, our processes were all in place, so what SKS needed most was a steady hand on the tiller. I asked the late Sitaram Rao, a competent and dedicated SKS board member, to take my place. Sitaram was a seasoned banker who had made a career shift to development. He was the right person to hold the fort while I reluctantly settled into Chicago to try and get my personal life back on track.

Starting in January of 2004, I worked full-time on writing up my dissertation; I had done my field research in India while working with SKS. With no income during this time, I began juggling credit card balances just to survive—I literally had an Excel spreadsheet showing how much debt I carried on each card, and when I needed to transfer balances.

I even seriously considered filing for personal bankruptcy, but I just couldn't reconcile it with the message of fiscal discipline I'd been preaching to our borrowers in India.

I had no choice but to put one foot in front of the other, hoping things would get better. The first step was to chip away at finishing my dissertation. Once I finished, I knew I'd be in a better position to find work. I also knew that, given my financial position, I couldn't afford to take a teaching or development job, which would have been my first choice.

For the first time in my life, I knew I'd have to take a job not for reasons of personal or professional commitment, but for the money. So I sought out the highest-paying job I could find in Chicago: an entry-level position at the management consulting firm McKinsey & Company. I didn't know much about management consulting, but if nothing else, I could also learn firsthand about *Fortune* 500 companies and how they run their businesses while also digging my way out of debt.

I applied and made it through three rounds of interviews, and in August of 2004, just after submitting my dissertation, I started work. Slowly, I began getting my life back on track.

It WAS SURREAL TO be an entry-level employee in a giant firm after having launched my own start-up, especially since many of my colleagues were freshly minted MBA graduates several years younger than me. Most were typical hustling young business types, competing to see who could log the most hours at the office, but I was just trying to do enough to survive. I'd start at McKinsey around 8 a.m., work all day long, then jump into SKS business starting around 10 p.m.—just as my colleagues in Chicago were packing up and the business day in India was getting started.

It was an insane schedule, but I wanted to stay as involved as possible with SKS. And of course, I was already used to working crazy hours from the first six years of getting SKS off the ground. The saving grace of spending all those hours toiling at McKinsey was the salary: I was making about $150,000 a year, typical for an MBA entry level, but far higher than anything I'd ever earned before. Slowly and painfully, I began to pull myself out of debt.

Meanwhile, on the other side of the world, we continued having to deal with unexpected and occasionally bizarre hurdles to our expansion. Even as I was spending my days in the antiseptic corporate environment of McKinsey, I was reminded in my nightly phone calls and periodic visits to India that it was a whole different world out there.

In late September of 2004, local gangsters in the town of Nizambad began attacking our loan officers. First, they tried to extort us, demanding to be paid a small amount of cash in exchange for a guarantee of safety in their district.

When we refused to pay, they launched a campaign of threats and intimidation: bands of thugs wielding broken bottles and machetes started attacking our loan officers, sometimes stealing their backpacks.

After a few such assaults, the gang approached our district manager again for a cash payment, obviously expecting us to accept their offer in exchange for our loan officers' safety. But to their surprise, we once again refused to give in. And since physical intimidation hadn't worked, they tried another tack, launching a campaign of rumors and lies to try and discredit us.

Nizambad is a largely Muslim area, so they began spreading rumors that SKS was a secret Christian organization, trying to convert everyone—they even falsely claimed to have found a Bible in one loan officer's backpack. In India, there's a grave sensitivity around Muslim issues. The 1947 partition of India, which created Pakistan as a separate Muslim state, was a bloody, long, and costly undertaking that ultimately claimed as many as a million lives. After partition, millions of Muslims continued to live in India, but raw feelings persisted on both sides, and even today, perceived attacks on the Muslim faith—from any source—arouse an instant and visceral reaction in India. This is especially true around Ramadan, the holiest period on the Muslim calendar. And unfortunately for us, these attacks in Nizambad happened to take place during Ramadan or, as it's known in India, Ramzan.

The more we resisted, the more the threats, attacks, and rumors intensified. One loan officer was forced to humiliate himself by stripping down to his underwear in a public square. Others were chased with machetes. We stopped sending loan officers to the hottest spots, but our members wanted their loans, so they started coming to our branch office to make repayments. They'd pool their money and send one member in an auto-rickshaw to deliver it to us.

At this point, we had the members on our side, even though they were Muslims too: they wanted their loans to continue, and they were resisting anti-SKS pressure as much as we were. We should have held a mass rally with our members then, to show others in the district that we had their support. But our local team was cowed by the continued threats, and unsure whether they could gather the momentum they needed. We missed our moment, and the gang seized its opportunity. They stepped up their intimidation even further, turning their attention directly to the members.

They threatened to forcibly cut our members' hair—a severe disgrace for Muslim women, who wear their hair long as proscribed by the Koran. This was too much for most of our members, many of whom gave in to the pressure, stopping their involvement and making no more repayments. We were hanging on by a thread, hoping to get things back on track, when the thugs launched their final blow—the one that would eventually make the newspapers back in the United States.

The gang went to the local Muslim leaders, claiming that SKS was a secret Christian evangelical group. They also complained about the fact that Muslims were taking loans from us—an act that is forbidden by the Koran. But although it's technically forbidden, MFIs and local moneylenders, including Muslim ones, had been offering loans in Muslim communities for years—even Bangladesh, where Muhammad Yunus started Grameen Bank, is a predominantly Muslim state. It was a technicality, but a compelling one for the Muslim clerics of Nizambad. So they issued a *fatwa,* or religious ruling, against SKS.

And that was the final straw. With a *fatwa* hanging over our heads, we were now an official nonentity in Nizambad, and any remaining support among our members vanished completely. We had no choice but to close that branch and walk away from the portfolio—nearly a quarter-million dollars in loans. This was an incredibly painful development, and not just financially; I knew our borrowers would suffer too, and we couldn't do anything to help them. I was still determined not to give in to extortion demands, but this was the perfect example of how taking that stand could, and did, harm us.

If the *fatwa* felt surreal, our confrontations with armed leftist rebels were even more so. In all the planning I'd done in the early days, figuring out how SKS would run and what our potential problems might be, I never anticipated having to face down shadowy groups of leftist guerrillas sending threatening messages from deep in the forests.

In parts of rural India, there are bands of armed rebels engaged in ongoing warfare against the Indian state. They're conducting what they believe is a revolution on behalf of the people of India, engaging in acts of violence and intimidation in an effort to destabilize the Indian government: in recent years, they have assassinated a state minister of home affairs, kidnapped corporate executives, and tried to kill a former chief minister with a bomb. The government considers them to be terrorists, and their groups have been outlawed in several Indian states. For this reason, they've retreated to secluded places, usually deep in forested areas where they have cover and isolation while planning their campaigns of violence.

Not surprisingly, the leftist rebels didn't take kindly to a capitalist organization like SKS spreading through rural India. Almost from the beginning, we saw signs that they were taking notice of our work; suffice it to say, they had ways of making their presence known. They started with indirect intimidation, such as stopping a loan officer and inquiring about his business, or popping up at a public meeting to say we were exploiting the villagers. But soon enough, they began employing more direct tactics, such as sending letters with block printing telling us to stop, or making threatening calls to our branch offices.

On one occasion, one group sent word that they wanted me to come to their hideaway in a dank back alley of Hyderabad. I was wary of going, but also, in my typically optimistic way, I thought I might be able to actually explain why we did what we did. We were giving poor Indians the tools to help themselves, after all—giving them a way to get out from under the thumb of crooked landlords and moneylenders. Wasn't this at least partially in line with the goals of a revolution for the people?

I agreed to the meeting, and the guerrillas sent instructions to meet at a certain street corner at a certain time. I took two SKS employees with me—a local area manager and an older employee who functioned as our designated troubleshooter. At the corner, we were met by a man who walked us down a maze of alleys to a nondescript house, then showed us into a bare-bones upstairs room with just a table and chairs. A couple of guerrillas were waiting for us there, and they got right to business.

They demanded extortion payments—everything from money to jeeps to AK-47 assault rifles. These weren't like the demands from local politicians, who could be dissuaded by appeals to higher-level public officials. The men sitting across from us were desperados, lawless types who fully expected to kill—and die—for what they believed. I could hardly believe this was even happening, but I told them the same thing I'd told the politicians: we would never make a payment to them, not even a rupee.

The leader leaned toward me, anger flashing across his face. With a sneer he told me all the ways his guerillas could harm me if we didn't do as they said. There would be mayhem, he told me, and no one would ever find the bodies. Did I really want to take that chance?

By now, I was shaking, though I tried not to let him see that. I was convinced he meant what he said, and I was afraid not just for my own safety, but for the safety of my employees. This was completely out of hand—these men were not kidding around, and I was the one who'd ultimately have to answer for putting SKS employees' lives at risk.

"Look," I told the man, "we're not going to give you anything. But if you're going to do something violent in retaliation, please make sure you do it to me." I took a piece of paper out of my bag and started scribbling on it. "Here's my address, and here's the license plate of my vehicle. Please leave everyone else, our staff members and borrowers, alone."

I pushed the paper across the table, and we stood to leave. My legs were trembling, but I managed to make it downstairs and out the door. I was convinced I was a dead man, and even told the two employees with me where I wanted to be buried—under a tree on the grounds of our first SKS branch—if the rebels killed me.

They didn't, of course. But I was filled with fear. Yet, in all honesty, despite being frightened, I think I still never believed real harm would come to me in any of these threatening confrontations. Somehow I had this optimism, a spiritual faith almost, that since I was doing good work and had good intentions, I would be protected—in the same way I'd felt protected when I was hitchhiking in the States during my college days.

But my standing up to these rebels was nothing compared to what a group of our borrowers did a couple of years later. Guerrillas had threatened to harm an SKS loan officer, telling him they'd kill him if he didn't accede to their demands to stop all SKS activity in the areas they controlled. At the next weekly meeting, the loan officer told his borrowers about the threat—and the women proceeded to do something truly extraordinary. One by one, they took a stand at the meeting and declared that they would defend him. Then, in an act of remarkable bravery, several of the women actually went to meet the guerillas at their camp in the forest. They told the guerrillas that before ever laying a hand on the loan officer, they would have to "take us first."

When I heard this story, I was incredibly moved. These women showed the kind of courage you rarely see in life. And they showed remarkable loyalty to SKS, which also touched me deeply. Yes, we were forced to face strange and sometimes frightening circumstances to grow our business. But as the bad times showed, we were doing so with extraordinary members and employees.

Despite the peaceful resolution of these two confrontations, the larger issue of making peace with the leftist rebels still exists. They, like us, adhere to strong, principled stands—it's just that their principles are very different from ours. Learning how to peacefully coexist in light of those differences is an ongoing challenge, and it is one that we still have not fully resolved.

IN LATE 2004, while still in Chicago and working for McKinsey, I began putting together an initial group of investors for a first round of investment. Six years after our launch, with more than forty thousand members and $10 million in cumulative loans disbursed, we had finally broken even. At last, it was time for SKS to make the switch from nonprofit to for-profit. And that meant we could begin raising much larger sums from investors, rather than scrambling for donations.

The first person I called was Ravi Reddy, the tech entrepreneur who had surprised me with a $50,000 donation back in 1998, and who had continued to support SKS in the years since. Ravi had always been drawn to our for-profit vision for SKS, and he, along with his partner Sandeep Tungare, were eager to become angel investors. He also helped me identify other investors who might be interested in stepping up.

I flew to San Francisco and made my way down highway 280 to Silicon Valley, the hub of venture capital in America. Once there, I made pitch after pitch to potential investors, telling them all the same thing: "The poor are entrepreneurial, and their businesses earn extraordinarily high returns. If you invest in SKS, we can invest in them—and fortunes will come to both of you." I put together a PowerPoint presentation and walked the VCs through an explanation of how SKS worked. And I told them we had a 99 percent payback rate among our poor customers.

At that time, in late 2004, microfinance was just beginning to make news—but it was still a little-understood business taking place a world away. Also, venture capitalists had been burned badly when the dot-com bubble burst a few years earlier, so they weren't as free with their money as they once had been. Even though a number of potential investors were intrigued, several told me the same thing: we're interested, but only if you return to the helm as CEO. The idea was that an early-stage venture investment was primarily a bet on the drive and the passion of an entrepreneur. The formula wouldn't work if I wasn't in India.

My divorce had been finalized, and my ex-wife had been granted custody of our young son. Even if I was in Chicago full time, the most I'd be able to see him was every other weekend and possibly one evening a week—the standard visitation schedule for divorced dads. And since I was often traveling during the week for McKinsey, I would be relegated to seeing my son only every other weekend.

Given those circumstances, I came up with another possible scenario: I would move back to India as SKS CEO, but as part of my new contract, the company would fly me back to Chicago every fourth week. My ex-wife could have my son three weeks in a row, but then I'd have him the fourth. I'd work twenty-one days straight, but then have seven days with my son, so I'd actually get to see him more each month than if I stayed in Chicago.

I'd been in the NGO mind-set for so long, this felt like an audacious thing to ask. But in a for-profit company, this wasn't an unreasonable request. Similarly, I knew I couldn't continue to survive on a nonprofit salary—my legal debts weren't paid off, and now I had a son to support—so I realized I needed to ask for a more corporate salary. With trepidation, I asked for an annual salary of $100,000. This was a huge pay cut from my McKinsey salary, but on the other hand, it was the largest salary for any head of an Indian microfinance institute.

My requests caused consternation among some of our initial investors. But another of our first-round investors was Vinod Khosla, a cofounder of Sun Microsystems who had made billions with the sale of Sun and become a partner at Kleiner, Perkins, Caufield & Byers, one of the most successful venture capital firms in the world. And he had something to say to the others about my salary request.

Vinod was probably the most influential Indian tech entrepreneur in America. Sun Microsystems, which he had cofounded with Scott McNealy and Andy Bechtolsheim, had changed the face of computing with its software, hardware, and IT services. I had spent two years trying to convince him to invest in SKS, but his answer had always been the same: "In principle, this is interesting," he'd tell me. "But I don't have the time to devote to it, and I don't like to put money into something I can't give time to."

"Well," I'd reply, "we've spent an hour together—what do you think that's worth?" Vinod would just smile wryly and shake his head. Eventually, I had worn Vinod down with constant appeals and growing evidence that SKS was a good bet. So at last, in 2005, he agreed to become an investor—with the caveat that I had to return as CEO.

But now I had to convince my first-round investors about my salary needs. I laid out my financial position and the situation with my son, and explained that I felt like this was the only solution. Various investors and I went back and forth over two weeks, until a phone conversation with Vinod finally tipped the balance.

I was in Washington, D.C., on McKinsey business, staying at the posh St. Regis Hotel near the White House. Vinod and I were on the phone, discussing the salary issue, when he asked me point-blank what my monthly expenses were in Chicago. I told him about child support, paying off debt, and the other general expenses I had. Finally, after a pause, he said, "Okay. We'll do it."

I was so relieved, I wanted to cry. As we had gone back and forth over the past few weeks, I'd felt my whole life was in the balance. I wanted nothing more than to be able to return to SKS—and this would allow me to do it, while still acting in a fiscally responsible way toward my son. Vinod went back to the other investors and said, "This is a reasonable salary for the CEO of a company of this size."

With Vinod's coaxing, the other investors got on board, and by the spring of 2005 the deal was done. Our first-round investment—from Vinod Khosla, Ravi Reddy, Sandeep Tungare, Unitus, and the Small Industries Development Bank of India—totaled $2.5 million. The parent nonprofit organization received significant "sweat equity" for having created the microfinance portfolio. This was allocated to trusts for the communities of SKS borrowers.

Some of my business friends said that I should be given this sweat equity, since I founded SKS. That was the way it worked in the for-profit world. But I felt that if a nonprofit creates value with donor funds, the value should go to the borrowers—the intended beneficiaries of the nonprofit. My view is that it would have been unethical for me to take any of the sweat equity personally.

In addition, Mike Murray, the chair of Unitus, personally paid down a chunk of my credit card debt. And finally, to my relief and excitement, I could now head back to India to resume being CEO of SKS.

As it turned out, I was returning just in the nick of time—because 2006 would be the year everything exploded.

CHAPTER SIX

Goat Economics

IN OCTOBER OF 2005, just two months after I returned to India to resume being CEO, I drove to the airport in Hyderabad to greet a VIP. Rahul Gandhi, the son of the late prime minister Rajiv Gandhi and the current Congress Party president Sonia Gandhi, was coming to Andhra Pradesh to pay SKS a visit. He had recently been elected to Parliament, and this was his first trip to our state since the election.

As a scion of the Nehru-Gandhi family, thirty-six-year-old Rahul was a big deal in India. An up-and-coming young politician who was trailed by a pack of news cameras everywhere he went, he was expected to become a serious contender for prime minister. About a month earlier, his chief of staff had called to say that Rahul wanted to see firsthand how microfinance worked, so we had made arrangements to take him out into the villages.

I got my first hint of what a big deal this was when the calls started coming in. Rahul's team had asked me to keep the visit confidential for security reasons—but slowly, word leaked out, and before long I was getting calls from government officials, the media, and senior politicians asking for details. I always refused, but when Rahul's arrival date came, the secret was out: more than ten thousand people came to the airport to see him.

I arrived at the airport and was escorted into the VIP lounge, where I was to receive Rahul before taking him out to the villages. As I entered the lounge, I walked past a line of politicians who were being made to wait behind a glass barrier. They couldn't quite believe I was being allowed in while they had to wait, and couple of them began complaining, saying things like, "I'm a minister—who is he?" Eventually, the security head asked me to leave the lounge because of the growing ruckus, and I was escorted directly out to the tarmac to receive Rahul, who came off the plane in jeans and a short-sleeved shirt and greeted me warmly. To my great satisfaction, I was then able to walk with Rahul right back past that same line of politicians, enjoying their surprised stares all the way.

We left the airport in a cavalcade of bulletproof vehicles. Because his grandmother, Indira Gandhi, and his father had both been assassinated, Rahul was always kept in a tight security bubble—and there was even more concern today, as the road we were taking was the same one where Maoist guerrillas had assassinated a senior minister of the state just a few years prior.

Which is why what happened next was even more astounding: just after we reached the outskirts of the city, Rahul told his driver to stop. "Everyone will recognize me if we drive up in this thing," he said to me. "Let's get into your vehicle instead." The security guards tensed up immediately, but Rahul just strolled from his bulletproof SUV over to one of ours and climbed in.

Rahul and I had a wide-ranging discussion during the two-hour drive to the villages. I explained our work using a PowerPoint presentation on my laptop, and he listened intently, asked thoughtful questions, and didn't have the usual stunned reaction when I mentioned our interest rates—he clearly had the sophistication to understand our approach. We also talked about poverty. What do the poor want? What are the challenges they face? What are their dreams and aspirations? Rahul seemed genuinely eager to learn.

As we neared the village, Rahul's team told him that huge crowds and media had gathered—somehow, even the details of where we were going had leaked. But Rahul was unperturbed. He simply turned to me and asked if we could go to a different village, explaining that if there were crowds and press, he wouldn't be able to see how things really were, which was the whole point.

I was amazed. I have to admit that when Rahul's chief of staff first asked about a village visit, I thought it would be little more than an attempt at building his image. But with this request, it was obvious that for Rahul, this trip wasn't about image. He wasn't seeking out press coverage—he wanted to truly understand what was going on in the country, from the ground up.

Eventually, we ended up staying at the first village, as the police were able to cordon off the crowds and press so Rahul could interact just with the villagers. He sat in on a center meeting, asked questions of our members, and even handed out a loan. After the meeting, we visited one borrower's hut, and she explained how she made money from her microenterprise, a milk-producing buffalo. She also told Rahul about her husband, who was a bonded laborer—a form of indentured servitude that still exists in India.

As the woman explained her husband's predicament of working essentially without pay, Rahul started asking more questions. Which landlord was he working for? How long had he been a bonded laborer? Where was he now? As he talked, I realized Rahul wanted to go to the farm where this laborer was bonded, and perhaps try and get him released. By this time, though, it was dusk, and the head of security was giving me alarmed looks, as he'd also realized what Rahul had in mind.

Once darkness fell, it would be easier for leftist guerillas to launch an attack, so the security head urged Rahul to return to Hyderabad. He relented, and as we pulled out of the village, he saw the thousands of people still standing outside the security cordon, hoping to catch a glimpse of him. "Stop the car," he said, then turned to me. "Give me a second. You've shown me your work; now I will show you mine." He jumped up on the roof of the SUV and began waving, as people in the crowd screamed wildly. After a few seconds, he hopped down and got back into the SUV, and we were off.

On the way back to Hyderabad, Rahul wanted to talk further, about everything from politics to economics to philosophy. At one point, he spoke of the need for people in the social sector to get more engaged with politics. "We have to get good people into politics," he said, looking straight at me. "Otherwise, we'll never have real change." As he spoke, I found myself intrigued at the idea of entering politics—but just as quickly, the feeling left me. The kind of political empowerment of the poor I had in mind would surely face resistance from vested political interests, and I just didn't have the stomach for engaging in the necessary compromises of Indian politics. Better, I thought, to build on relationships with progressive politicians like

Rahul Gandhi, to influence government policies from the outside in.

As we approached the city, Rahul asked whether I had dinner plans. I took him to Paradise, a restaurant that specialized in the famous Hyderabad *biryani*, and we talked through a long dinner. I finally dropped him off at 11:30 that night.

Images from Rahul's visit to Andhra Pradesh dominated India's news cycle the next day, accompanied by front-page articles on SKS—who we were, what we did, how our program worked. For the first time, ordinary Indians across the country were hearing about us. We were already making a name for ourselves in the rural areas we served, but this was the beginning of a much wider recognition. And as we now moved into a period of hypergrowth, SKS was positioning itself for the next leap: becoming a household name.

WHEN I RESIGNED AS CEO in January of 2004, we had about 25,000 members. By the time I returned in August of 2005, we had grown to 120,000. This was a phenomenal growth rate by any measure, yet it had all gone surprisingly smoothly. A big reason for that was the stellar leadership of Sitaram Rao and the passion of Praseeda Kunam, a young, driven firebrand who really stepped up at SKS during my absence. But while we'd grown rapidly, we hadn't yet reached the exponential growth we'd need to achieve our vision of scaling microfinance beyond what anyone had ever done before.

We knew that one big challenge to adding so many new members would be finding—and training—enough managers to serve them all. At the time, the typical microfinance model of recruiting and training field staff was an apprentice model, where new loan officers would work for four to five months and then be deployed to the field. But if we wanted to grow at the pace we envisioned, that training was far too long.

How could we accelerate the process? We decided to look to the example of franchise companies like McDonald's and Burger King, as they've had great success in quickly training and deploying large, unskilled work forces. We enlisted the help of a British franchising consultant, and the top field staff and I sequestered ourselves for a week, writing up a step-by-step manual that would describe in painstaking detail every single process our loan officers would use.

At the end of the week, we emerged with an extremely detailed manual and a streamlined two-month training process for loan officers—tools that would help us train up to a thousand new loan officers a month, many of whom came to us with little experience handling money and numbers. We modeled our process on "Hamburger University," the renowned McDonald's training facility where new franchisees learn everything about how to run a fast-food restaurant the McDonald's way.

Under our eight-week program, each fresh SKS recruit—typically a recent high school graduate—takes a weekly theory class, then spends five days a week in the field shadowing a loan officer. Initially, the recruits learn by watching, but gradually they take on responsibilities themselves, learning by doing. By the end of the training, they already have hands-on experience and can seamlessly transition to work as loan officers—thereby solving the problem of how to add hundreds of new loan officers quickly.

From this rapidly growing pool, we could promote and train the next two levels: branch managers and district managers. But there was still one more problem to solve. How could we quickly find and train area managers, the higher-level employees who would each supervise twenty-five branches, with a member base of more than one hundred thousand? These positions required recruits with much more advanced skill sets.

At this point, the conventional thinking in microfinance was to bring in managers with ten or more years of work experience, then train them for six months or more. But bringing in such experienced staff was costly, and seasoned people sometimes come with baggage—stubbornly conventional thinking about how things should be done, based on their "experience." Also, even though an area manager's work was more complex than that of a loan officer, we couldn't afford to take six months to train them. Our plans called for an aggressive expansion from Andhra Pradesh into multiple Indian states, so we needed new area managers immediately. But how could we identify, hire, and train highly capable people quickly, and at a low cost?

The answer to the first problem solved the second one as well. Rather than hiring older, more experienced recruits, I decided to go in the opposite direction: A couple of months before returning as CEO, I asked Praseeda to hire four recent management graduates, the Indian equivalent of MBAs. In India, such students study management right after their undergraduate work, so we basically had four "kids"—all in their early to mid-twenties, and all eager to start their first jobs.

People were surprised and a little dubious about this approach, with one MFI leader even saying point-blank that those types of recruits couldn't cut it. But I had reasons of my own for believing that relatively inexperienced young people could do such high-level work. "Just because they're young doesn't mean they can't do it," I told my colleague. "I was young at DDS, too, but I just needed some guidance and trust."

The four young people Praseeda had hired began their training in May of 2005, but three months later, when I arrived in India to resume being CEO, all four were still working in Andhra Pradesh. "This wasn't the idea," I told

Praseeda. "We need to send them out to the new states." She knew that had been my intention, but while I was away, she just couldn't bring herself to send these inexperienced kids out to run multiple branches in brand-new territories. It felt like too great a risk—one Praseeda wasn't willing to take.

But I was. I immediately called the four young people into a meeting and said, "You're each going to run an area, and you're going to do it in different states. We're expanding, and you're going to lead the way." I unfurled a map of India and laid it on the table in front of them. "Okay," I said. "So, who wants to work in which state? Anyone?" The four young faces before me looked absolutely blank.

"Come on," I said. "Speak up! Don't be shy!" I pointed to a young man in the front. "Where do you want to go?"

"Really?" he asked. "Just pick one? Just like that?"

"Yes," I said, growing impatient. "Look, do you want to be an apprentice for the rest of your life? Didn't you study management so you could be a CEO one day?" I looked around at the four of them; they seemed a bit shell-shocked. "Now's your chance to actually run something," I said. "So, let's go! Pick your state." One by one, the four chose their states, and within a few weeks they had all relocated.

Yes, this was risky—but we didn't have time to second-guess ourselves. And at this point, my experience at McKinsey came into play: before spending that year at McKinsey, I had never spent time with executives of *Fortune* 500 companies. I had this vague notion that there was some kind of magic to what they did, because they were so large and successful, and I considered myself a novice in comparison. But the more time I spent with them, the more I realized that we really *did* know what we were doing at SKS. And in some cases, we were functioning at a higher and more efficient level than these big, global companies. Seeing that gave me a lot more confidence in my own abilities when I returned as CEO.

The simple truth was, we had to expand quickly, and this was the most efficient way to do it. I knew that if we could find young people as determined and eager as I had been in my days at DDS, it would work. I had faith in these young people, even if they didn't yet have it in themselves. And my hunch was rewarded: very quickly, SKS became one of the leading MFIs in every one of the states where we'd sent our new young area managers.

The next year, we hired twenty management graduates, ramping up our growth even more. This time around, we designed an accelerated two-month training like the one we'd created for loan officers, so we could get them into the field even quicker. The program was so successful that in the years to come, we increased our numbers of young people hired to be area managers, finally topping out at recruiting nearly a hundred a year.

With our recruitment and training up to speed, our software streamlining our recordkeeping, and $2.5 million of equity solving our capital needs, I now had one goal for SKS: to grow, grow, grow, as fast as we could. This was the moment I'd been aiming for all these years. It was time to show everyone—other MFIs, investors, politicians, NGOs—that we could practice microfinance in a way that would serve more poor people than anyone had ever thought possible.

THE YEAR 2006 BROUGHT THE perfect storm: a sharp spike in our growth, plus increased worldwide awareness of microfinance, plus the rising profile for SKS that started with the Rahul Gandhi visit all led to an explosion of attention. If 2004 had been the most difficult year of my life, 2006 soon became the most rewarding.

In March, SKS signed up its 200,000th member, with a total of 400,000 people—members and their spouses—covered by our life insurance product. I set an ambitious goal of "7 by 7"—700,000 members by March 2007—and announced it publicly, which turned a lot of heads in the microfinance world. For years, SKS had been the aggressive young upstart that talked a big game but had yet to reach it. Now, we were reaching it—and beyond.

A couple of weeks later, I received an invitation to an event to be hosted by *Time* magazine, honoring "The 100 People Who Shape Our World." Each spring, the magazine named its list of the one hundred most influential people of the year, and at first I thought I was simply being invited to a cocktail party. But when I got a call from a reporter soon afterward, I realized with a shock that I was being included on the list. This was beyond my wildest imaginings—SKS was still only the third-largest MFI in India, but the *Time* editors had chosen me.

When the issue hit the newsstands on May 1, 2006, I was one of two Indians on the list—the other was the co-founder of the computer giant Infosys, Nandan Nilekani. We joined such luminaries as Bill Clinton, Bill and Melinda Gates, Bono, Oprah Winfrey, and Al Gore on the list. I could hardly believe it was true until I bought the magazine in a shop and flipped through to see my photo. And no one else seemed to believe it either—throughout the day, Indian TV stations flashed photos of Nandan and me, most often accompanied by the caption, "Who is Vikram Akula?" But after this *Time* article, that wouldn't be a question in India anymore.

Two weeks later, in its May 15, 2006, issue, the *Wall Street Journal* ran a front-page story about me. It detailed how and why I started SKS and what we were aiming to accomplish, reaching a whole new constituency of people, further raising our profile, and arousing even more interest in our ideas about aggressively for-profit microfinance. Suddenly, everyone wanted to learn about microfinance and how we practiced it. And that included two of the richest people in the world, whom I met with that very week.

The Gates Foundation was considering launching its own microfinance funding program, and Bill and Melinda Gates, as was their habit when entering a new sector, were trying to learn everything possible about it. Melinda Gates had come to India six months earlier to see microfinance in action, visiting villages and holding discussions with Indian microloan providers, including me. The next step after her field visits was convening a global roundtable: the foundation invited eight MFI practitioners from all over the world to fly in and meet with Bill and Melinda at their offices in Seattle.

The eight of us were shown into a plain conference room in a nondescript (but, as I was later told, bulletproof) building. We'd been told that Melinda and Bill would be joined by his father, Bill Gates Sr., as well as a "friend" of theirs. That friend turned out to be Warren Buffett. When the four of them walked into the room, we all stood as if on cue. Nobody planned it, but I think we all felt a bit overwhelmed at meeting with some of the most powerful business and philanthropic minds in the world. And they were here to learn from us.

I had an even more surreal moment when Melinda introduced everyone around the table. When she got to me, she had barely gotten out the words, "This is Vikram Akula—" before Warren Buffett jumped in, saying, "I know who you are. I just read about you in the *Journal*." I smiled and nodded, incredulous that the most influential investor in the world had just read about *me* in the *Wall Street Journal*.

We launched into a wide-ranging discussion, explaining the basics of microfinance, the differences in how it's practiced in various parts of the world, and the structure developed by Muhammad Yunus back in the 1970s. Melinda was the facilitator, as she'd met all of us already, but Buffett and Bill Gates took active part, too. Then suddenly, Bill leaned back in his chair, his brow furrowed.

"But hold on," he said. "There's one thing I don't get."

He peered through his glasses, looking straight at me. "What are people possibly doing," he asked, "where they can pay 28 percent interest on a loan and still make money?"

I had answered this question many times before, but never to the world's richest man. I pulled myself up in my chair, took a deep breath and responded with an example: "Say you have a landless agricultural laborer," I began. "Even though she owns absolutely nothing, she can take a loan of, say, two thousand rupees—about forty dollars. She can use that money to buy a goat. She can then take that goat with her to work when she goes to the fields. The goat eats virtually anything along the way, so there's no investment from her side to feed it—she just takes it to the fields, ties it up while she's working, and then walks it back home when she's done."

As Bill Gates scribbled notes on the pad in front of him, I went on. "A goat typically gives birth twice a year—usually two kids per birth, but sometimes only one. So, even in the conservative scenario, if the goat gives birth twice and gives only one kid each time, you've got two offspring," I said. "And the value of each offspring is usually about 50 percent of that of the mother goat.

"So by the end of the year, you've got 100 percent return. You've got the mother goat, worth two thousand rupees, and two kids, worth a thousand each. Even if you took out the cost of capital at 28 percent of the loan, you're making in the range of 70-plus percent return on invested capital." Bill looked up from his pad. "The laborer can pay the weekly loan installment from her work in the fields, or if needed she can sell the kids for cash and still have a significant asset—a mother goat worth two thousand rupees— that she can sell later."

This standard explanation of what I call "goat economics" seemed to impress him, but I wasn't finished yet. I went on to explain that this is a typical scenario with microenterprises—they tend to yield extraordinarily high returns, for four reasons. First, and most important, they most often use family labor, which is far more productive than hiring wage laborers. Think of your classic immigrant-owned grocery store in the United States, with sons and daughters providing the bulk of the labor. It's both more productive and cheaper than hiring others to do your work for you.

Second, in the "informal economy," micro-entrepreneurs don't have to pay any legal fees or taxes—making it much easier, and quicker, to turn a profit. Third, poor entrepreneurs have very few infrastructure costs. A village grocery, for example, is a home-front store, not a separate place that requires extra infrastructure costs. And fourth, for the preceding three reasons, capital represents only a small percentage of the new venture's overall input. Capital is a catalyst, no doubt, but the fundamental economics of microbusiness really aren't significantly impacted by the interest rates. What's far more important is timely access to capital.

For all these reasons, the poor are able to make good money, even with high-interest-rate loans. "Though 28 percent might seem high," I said, "the demand among poor Indians for our loans has exploded, and we have almost no defaults among borrowers. At SKS, we have a 99.4 percent payback rate—much higher than the rate of Western loan paybacks." The conclusion was obvious—the system is working for the poor. And there was no reason it couldn't continue to work, for borrowers, investors, and lenders.

As I finished my explanation of goat economics, I watched Bill Gates scribble a few more notes on his pad. At that moment, a thought popped into my head: "I'm explaining to the world's richest man how the world's poorest people make money on goats." It was an amazing moment, one that pretty well summed up that amazing year.

But of all the attention we got in 2006, the most important wasn't from newspapers or magazines or even Bill

Gates. The most important was from investors, who suddenly began to see SKS not just as an interesting play in the microfinance world, but as a solid, rapidly growing business with a tremendous profit potential.

THE CALLS STARTED COMING in May, just after the *Time* and *Wall Street Journal* articles put us on the map. Bankers and venture capitalists began reaching out, asking for meetings and field visits, and saying things like, "Don't go anywhere else for money, Vikram. We'll give you whatever you need."

This was brand-new territory for me. After years of having to convince donors and investors to take a chance on us, we suddenly had an influx of wealthy suitors. I didn't really know the language of venture investing, and I didn't even know who some of the major players were. In August of 2006, when we got a call from Sequoia Capital—one of the largest venture capital firms in Silicon Valley—an adviser at Unitus, one of our early investors, had to tell me to meet with them.

I was pretty naive about how venture investing worked at this level, so I just went with the flow, trying not to let on whenever I was confused about something. In one meeting with Citibank in Mumbai about raising debt, I listened patiently as one of their people talked about "dirty paper" and "clean paper"—financial terms that everyone in the room seemed to know but which meant nothing to me. I just nodded my head, looking serious and attentive, wondering what in the world those terms could mean.

In other ways, my naivete actually helped. Once word got out that Sequoia was interested, other firms came calling, and soon we had about a dozen potential suitors. This was perfect, I thought—we could hold a bake-off, see who would offer us the best deal and pick and choose as we pleased. I didn't realize this wasn't how things were done in the world of venture capital, so I just happily forged ahead, essentially asking these investors to impress us, rather than the other way around.

When the Sequoia team came to India for a field visit, I scheduled an unnecessarily early time for heading out into the villages. "We'll come pick you up at 6 a.m.!" I told the team, thinking to myself that their level of enthusiasm for getting up so early would show me how enthusiastic they were about the business—and the investment. I wanted to test them, to see how dedicated they were to our mission. On the other hand, I didn't really worry about impressing them, as I knew our business model was solid and our growth potential huge. To my mind, it would be obvious to everyone why they'd want to invest with us.

And my hunch was correct: at the end of the field visit, Sumir Chadha of Sequoia turned to me and said, "We'd like to make an investment." He rattled off a "premoney valuation figure," and once again I didn't know exactly what that meant, so I just nodded sagely and said nothing. I couldn't wait to find out what that offer actually represented.

As it turned out, figuring out our valuation was the biggest question we had to answer. Whoever ultimately invested in SKS would receive a percentage of the company's stock in return, so to figure out that percentage we had to determine how much the company was worth overall. But how could we possibly assess that number accurately? In the fiscal year ending March 2006, we had only $100,000 in profits—but we were also growing at a breakneck pace. By August of 2006, we had about three hundred thousand members and nearly $75 million in loans disbursed, and we were on track to more than double the number of borrowers when the fiscal year ended in March 2007, and reach beyond 2 million the year after that.

Much of the value of the company lay in its potential for growth, and no other MFIs were aiming to grow as fast as we were. How do you put a figure on that? There really wasn't any other model to compare us to.

With all the attention swirling around, we decided to invite bids from ten of the VC firms, banks, and private equity groups that had expressed interest. We sent financial statements and a business plan to each of them, and gave them seven days to respond in writing with a proposal. This, too, was incredibly unorthodox, but it worked: eight of the ten responded, and their valuations of the company ranged from $10 million to $18 million.

It would have been easy to simply choose the investor who gave SKS the highest valuation, but there were other factors to consider. Which group could best give us strategic guidance on hypergrowth? Who could open up doors to different kinds of debt financing, or connect us with vendors and business partners? In the end, we liked Sequoia very much—but their valuation wasn't the highest. Not wanting to leave money on the table, I decided to go back to Sequoia and ask them to meet the highest valuation. The way I saw it, if we could get them to match the numbers we wanted, we'd be all set.

A few of my friends and advisers thought this was, finally, pushing it too far. Entrepreneurs just didn't treat VCs as the supplicants! I was doing everything backward, and this, they feared, could be the last straw. But I was determined to get the number I wanted from the investor I wanted. We set up a meeting, and I essentially said to Sequoia, "This is the deal we want." They didn't hesitate, matching our number on the spot.

We finalized the deal with a handshake in December 2006: Sequoia would be the lead investor for an $11.5 million round of financing. We might not have entirely known what we were doing—in fact, the whole process had been so unusual that Harvard Business School wrote up a case study for use in its classes—but we had done it. We were attracting the big money now, which would further fuel our growth, leading to more investments and more growth, and eventually an initial public offering. Our aggressively for-profit business plan was working, and we'd be able to help more poor people than ever.

But within the microfinance community, not everyone was so thrilled. Muhammad Yunus, who won the Nobel Peace Prize that year for his pioneering work in microfinance, had long been a vocal critic of aggressively for-profit MFIs such as ours. With his new platform as a Nobel Prize winner, he ramped up his criticism. And with our new visibility, thanks to the investment and the press coverage, we were a natural target—although Yunus never criticized us directly. Suddenly, the debate about nonprofit microfinance versus aggressively for-profit microfinance turned hotter than ever.

This great debate hinged on one question: was making a profit from lending to the poor the equivalent of exploiting the poor? In the view of Yunus and others, it was. They believed the only ethical way to lend to the poor was to charge interest rates that just covered expenses, plus a small profit to encourage some growth. But inviting investments from large venture capitalists, as SKS was doing, and promising investors healthy returns—that was considered exploitation. In a 2006 *New Yorker* article, Yunus had this to say about the idea of making profits off lending to the poor: "When they have enough flesh and blood in their bodies, go and suck them, no problem. But until then, don't do that."

One reason there's so much unease about for-profit microfinance is that some MFIs, notably in Latin America, have charged extremely high interest rates—sometimes over 100 percent. One, Compartamos Bank, routinely charged around 85 percent, and reportedly gave its field agents bonuses for disbursing larger loans and maintaining high repayment rates—something SKS has never done, and will never do. When Compartamos had an IPO in April of 2007, raising $467 million for 30 percent of the company and enriching several private investors, critics on all sides assailed the company for predatory lending practices. As Muhammad Yunus put it in *Business Week*, "When you discuss microcredit, don't bring Compartamos into it. Microcredit was created to fight the moneylender, not to become the moneylender."

Yunus argues that MFIs should seek their capital from either donors or social investors, who would be content with just getting their principal back—and thus not requiring MFIs to charge high interest rates. This concept is intriguing, but by Yunus's own account, the pool of donor funds and social capital is quite limited. The pool of non-return-seeking funds that's currently allocated to microfinance falls far short of the $250 billion or so equity and debt needed to provide finance for the world's poor.

Clearly, there's not enough donor capital out there. But what about other sources? Is there any other pool of cash that would be sufficient to meet the MFIs' needs, while allowing them to charge minimal interest rates? There is—but the catch is, we're not allowed to use it.

If MFIs could create and access savings deposits for the poor, we'd have no need for external commercial capital (while also providing the poor with a much-needed cash-flow-smoothing product). But unfortunately, most countries don't allow MFIs to take deposits from the poor. Grameen Bank overcame this problem by becoming a bank for the poor through a special act of Bangladesh's parliament, but for most MFIs in most countries, there's no way to mobilize savings deposits.

Because of these limitations, the hard truth is this: the only place where MFIs can get enough capital to meet their lending needs is through commercial markets. And the only way to get commercial capital is by offering high profits in return. Investors won't invest unless they see a very large upside potential, because they see microfinance as risky—as unsecured loans to poor women who have no credit history and who are often illiterate. Small profits, in their view, just aren't worth the risk involved.

If all MFIs took the Yunus route, they'd never get the capital needed to achieve the exponential growth required to serve all the poor who need loans. And achieving that scale is the single most pressing need today—nothing else even comes close. Because every day that we can't afford to offer a loan to a poor person is a day that person remains unnecessarily mired in poverty.

For all these reasons, I'd argue that not only is it ethical for microfinance institutions to earn high profits, it's actually *more* ethical than practicing nonprofit microfinance.

Yet my stance on this question still seems to surprise some people, who apparently expect me to be embarrassed by our for-profit goals. Once, in a meeting with a group of senior bureaucrats, one accosted me, asking with great indignation, "We've heard you are charging 24 percent interest on your loans! What do you have to say to that?"

He clearly expected me to backpedal or apologize, but instead I drew myself up with equal indignation. "Sir," I barked back. "You are absolutely wrong. We do *not* charge 24 percent interest. Absolutely not.

"In fact, we charge 28 *percent*," I declared. "And let me explain why." The bureaucrat's expression changed from smug to startled, but I was happy to take this opportunity to explain how our rate structure worked.

I explained that because we weren't allowed to take savings deposits, we had to borrow money from commercial banks at around 11 percent. Furthermore, it was extremely costly to use a vast network of field officers to deliver tiny loans to members in tens of thousands of remote villages across India—about 12 percent of the loan amount. Finally, central bank regulations required we set aside 2 percent for potential defaults, leaving us about a 3 percent profit margin—the minimum needed to attract commercial investors.

I went on to explain that, even at 28 percent interest, ours was the lowest-cost financing available to the poor. Loan sharks charged more, commercial banks didn't exist in rural India, and going to a government bank would mean several trips for borrowers—each one involving bus fares, lost wages, food expenses, fees for the broker who would assist with the application, and even bribes that had to be paid to the bankers. A World Bank survey of India's poor indicated that they pay bribes as high as 10 to 20 percent of their government bank loans.

By the time I finished, most—though not all—in the room were convinced. The fact is, some people will never feel comfortable discussing poor people and profit in the same sentence, no matter how much sense it makes.

But I believe that a commercial approach is the best way to give the most poor people access to finance. My early days at DDS taught me a crucial lesson: the poor are really no different from you or me. They're not stupid or slow, and they aren't looking for us to rescue them or teach them anything. The relationship between SKS and our members is mutually beneficial. Our members are receiving tools that have long been denied them, and using them to do things they're naturally skilled at doing. In return, SKS is building an enormous member base, establishing a brand, raising money in investments, and continuing to expand the number of poor members served. It's a perfect circle, one that benefits everyone.

The notion that it's somehow unethical to enter into a profitable business working with the poor is insulting to the poor. They are not children who need our protection. They're working women and men who are thriving under a system that allows them to take their economic lives into their own hands. Treating them as anything less is unjust.

So, does that mean it's okay to charge extremely high interest rates such as those of Compartamos? No. There's a big difference between charging the highest interest rate you think the market will bear, as Compartamos has done, and charging rates that allow for continued expansion without pushing the market to its limit. The truth is, SKS could charge far higher interest rates than we do, and still have overwhelming demand. Remember, the alternatives for most poor Indians are moneylenders and loan sharks—or not being able to get loans at all, and falling into either landless labor or unemployment.

We don't believe in either the Grameen approach or the Compartamos approach. Instead, we have a third way. It's not simply a middle ground of moderate rates and moderate profits; it's something entirely different. It's an approach that simultaneously yields both low interest rates and high profits for investors. How do we do it? The answer lies in what I call Google territory.

CHAPTER SEVEN

Google Territory

AN INDIAN FOLKTALE CALLED "One Grain of Rice" tells the story of Rani, a girl who lives in a village of rice farmers. The *raja*, or king, decrees that everyone should deliver all their rice to be kept in the royal storehouses, in case of famine. When times are good, all is well—the raja metes out enough rice for everyone and keeps the rest in reserve. But when famine strikes the land, the greedy raja goes back on his promise, refusing to feed the villagers.

The raja keeps all the rice for himself, even as the villagers grow hungrier and hungrier. One day, he even makes plans for a great feast for himself, although the villagers are starving. He orders a servant to transport rice from the storehouses to the palace, and along the way the servant drops a few grains—which a young girl named Rani quickly picks up.

Instead of keeping the rice for herself, Rani delivers it to the raja, saying, "This belongs to you." Touched by her display of loyalty, the raja says he will give her whatever she asks in return.

"Please, just give me one grain of rice today," Rani replies. "One today, and two tomorrow, and four the next day." The raja nods, and she goes on. "For thirty days, sir, that is all I ask. Just double the number of grains each day for thirty days." The raja consents.

Rani knew what he did not: that doubling the number of grains may not seem much in the beginning, but by the thirtieth day, the raja would have to give her more than a billion grains of rice—the entire contents of the storehouses.

I like that folktale because it shows the power of numbers. And the power of numbers is what makes the incredible scale SKS has achieved over the last twelve years not simply a great microfinance business, but a different kind of business altogether. It's what allows us to reach Google territory.

I F A COMPANY MAKES A penny or two on a product it sells to a small number of people, it will never make much money. But if a company makes a few pennies on each product, and it sells fifteen to twenty products to tens of millions of people—that's when it starts to make real money. This is how Google has become so huge—by having an enormous constituency of "eyeballs" and making a little bit of money from multiple advertisements targeted to these huge numbers.

When SKS achieved a critical mass of more than a million members across India, with channels for product distribution already in place, we opened up a whole new world of possible revenue streams. And just as important, we opened up new opportunities for our members: great deals on goods and services, increased political power, and health and education initiatives that would have been impossible to undertake with smaller numbers. As much as SKS has grown over the past twelve years, this is really just the beginning. We—and more importantly, our members—are only now starting to reap the benefits of those numbers.

Historically, India's rural markets have been very hard to reach. The country's infrastructure is underdeveloped, so roadways are poor. It has never been cost-effective for companies to travel deep into rural areas to sell their products or services, as the cost of doing so invariably exceeds the revenue produced.

But SKS has already established highly functioning distribution channels, since our loan officers travel to remote

157

villages every single week, meeting with members regularly and developing relationships. With those channels firmly in place, we can use them for distributing other goods and services. There really is a "fortune at the bottom of the pyramid," as the late author and professor C.K. Prahalad wrote in his influential 2004 book of that title—and we are perfectly poised to tap into it.

This is why our "third way" works. Because our member base is so large, we can source goods and services for them at a very low cost. We can also offer suppliers our channels to market and distribute those goods and services, making it cost-effective for them to do so. With the savings on both ends, the costs to members are extremely low, even after we add a small financing charge for purchases. So the supplier gets a small margin on a large number of goods sold, and SKS can earn a small margin on its finance charge—which ultimately results in high profits because of the size of our member base. Everybody wins.

Here's an example: more than a million of our members have used their loans to open and run small home-front grocery, or *kirana* stores, where they sell things like toothpaste, soap, shampoo, and food items. The store owners make money from their new businesses, and their fellow villagers benefit by having greater access to goods.

So far so good. But here's the problem: the poor still pay disproportionately more than the rest of the world for their goods. If you buy a two-gallon jug of laundry detergent at your local grocery store, you're paying far less per wash than a poor person who buys little foil packets, called sachets, with individual servings of detergent. Buying in bulk always results in savings, but the poor don't have the cash flow to pay for so much of an item all at once. Additionally, by the time those single-serving sachets make it from the supplier through multiple middlemen, the price has been marked up several times over. The resulting high per-unit price of such goods is one reason why the poor have a harder time pulling themselves out of poverty.

But with hundreds of thousands of these SKS-funded kirana stores operating across the country, why not create a de facto national chain, increasing the storeowners' power and giving them access to cheaper bulk goods, direct from the supplier? Why not, in other words, create the equivalent of a grassroots Wal-Mart across India?

In the fall of 2008, I found myself sitting in front of a well coiffed, pinstripe-suited man with a British accent who could help us achieve this goal. His name was James Scott, and he was the Asia region head of Metro Cash & Carry, the European equivalent of the wholesaler Costco. His company had been trying to get into India for years, but they'd faced numerous obstacles, bureaucratic and otherwise. He'd come to realize that, while Metro might be able to serve some of the high-end retail customers directly, they couldn't break into the vast potential of small kirana stores on their own—they'd need to partner with someone who already had a foothold among the tens of millions of potential customers.

James was a captain of industry, but his eyes lit up as I started telling him about our members' tiny village kiosk grocery stores. "We have half a million stores across India," I said (the number has since risen), and you could practically see him doing mental calculations. It was a funny scene—James in his bespoke suit, representing a giant German conglomerate, and me in my *kurta* pajama shirt and sandals, making a business deal on behalf of hundreds of thousands of poor women.

Under our pilot program with Metro, SKS members with kirana stores can buy goods directly from the wholesaler. Instead of paying a high commission to a middleman in the local town, who might be selling whatever he can get his hands on, the kirana store owners now have standard, high-quality, branded goods—at a much cheaper price than they've been paying. And Metro has a way in to the gigantic market that has so far eluded them. All this is possible only because of the number of members we have—numbers we never could have reached operating as a nonprofit MFI. Everybody wins.

Similarly, through a deal with Nokia and Airtel, we've been able to finance cell phones for our members at rates cheaper than those normally available. The demand for cell phones in rural areas is extremely high, but the market had reached a saturation point: middle-class people who wanted phones already had them. And the poor who wanted them couldn't afford them. The cell phone companies knew there was a giant unfulfilled market out there—but there was no way to access those customers without incurring costs that exceeded the potential revenue.

So we approached Nokia and Airtel with a proposal, offering to use our branches and loan officers to take orders and hand-deliver phones. This was a huge opportunity for them, as it eliminated the costs that had kept them from expanding into this market. In return for this distribution, Nokia offered our members handsets at a steep discount, and Airtel offered a significant reduction on the cost of minutes. SKS financed the purchase, and just like that, tens of thousands of rural poor got access to cell phones they couldn't previously afford, while the phone companies got a whole new client base. Once again, we brokered a deal in which everybody wins.

IN SOME CASES, REACHING THE vast market of the rural poor involves more than just taking advantage of distribution channels. Because the needs of the poor are different from the needs of the middle and upper classes, entire product lines must be reconsidered. This was another lesson I learned from my earliest days at DDS: we needed to ask the poor directly what worked for them, rather than trying to force them into buying existing products that were designed for people in completely different circumstances.

The best example of this was our search for an endowment life insurance product for the poor.

Historically, poor Indians have been almost entirely uninsured—a real impediment to moving up the economic ladder. We wanted to change this, to offer products that would protect borrowers and their families in the event of illness or death. This was actually our first step in exploring what other products we could distribute—when you're already offering loans, it's easy enough to prepare another kind of paperwork for another kind of product, which the loan officers could then offer to our borrowers in their weekly meetings. So we started with term credit–life insurance, then health insurance, then explored an endowment or whole-life product.

Our experience with the endowment insurance was telling. Almost immediately, we ran into the first problem: existing insurance products didn't really work for the poor, who have different needs than more economically and socially stable groups. One insurer I met with asked me flat out, "How do you sell insurance to poor people?" But he was asking the wrong question. We didn't need to convince the poor to buy insurance products. After all, given their vulnerability to calamities like drought or illness, the poor are extremely attuned to risk. Instead, we needed to ask a different question: what kind of product can we design that will meet the needs of the poor?

Our loan officers began asking members what they needed and wanted in an endowment product. For one thing, they told us that typical premium rates were too high for them. Another big problem was that they were often scammed by insurers who canceled policies after missed payments. If you've been putting money into a policy for months, or even years, and the whole thing gets canceled upon a few missed payments, you've just thrown your money—hard-earned, desperately needed money—down a hole.

Our loan officers saw poor women pull out tattered old policy documents, asking if we could do anything about their lapsed policies. But it was too late for them. Crooked insurance agents, who knew the poor were very likely to miss payments now and then, had simply absconded with their money. So the insurance industry, in the experience of many poor Indians, was nothing but a scam.

We set about trying to come up with a product that suited the needs of the poor: we needed a policy that would be cheap, no more than 20 rupees (about 50 cents US) per week, and that would never lapse—even if members missed payments. These were strict demands for an insurer to meet, but on the other hand, marketing and distribution were already taken care of, which would take a huge burden off the insurance company.

Still, most insurers laughed us out of their offices when we proposed our model. But one, Bajaj Allianz, was visionary enough to say yes. This company leapt into these untested waters with us—and its endowment product for the poor became one of the most profitable parts of its business. Now we're working with Bajaj Allianz to design livestock, property, disability, home, and a host of other insurance products that help our members, all of which will make a profit thanks to the vast numbers we serve. Once again, everybody wins.

As SKS expanded to more villages and offered more products, we became one of the best-known brands in rural India. Kids in villages mimicked our role-playing games, offering imaginary loans to each other. Potential loan officer recruits would call when they heard we were starting in a new place. And potential members came to our branch offices, asking us to start up in their villages. We knew SKS was earning its place as a trusted brand, but we didn't realize just how far we'd come until the giant insurer ING did a survey of villagers' opinions.

In 2004, ING's national head of alternative channels, M. R. Rao, approached SKS to explore being a partner to sell insurance in areas where we worked. But first he wanted to see if the SKS brand was strong enough— whether members would buy insurance policies from us. He started out by asking villagers if they would consider buying insurance products. Then, he asked them which they'd prefer—insurance from SKS, ING, or the well-known state-run Life Insurance Corporation of India (LIC).

In villages where SKS was active, our members responded that they preferred an SKS product to the others. Rao wasn't surprised, as our members might be expected to show brand loyalty. But then he asked villagers who *weren't* SKS members—and they said the same thing. Of the three offered, villagers overwhelmingly preferred an SKS product, whether they were our members or not.

When Rao realized the extent to which SKS had penetrated the rural market, he didn't simply rethink his strategy for ING. He left the company altogether, and came to work for SKS as our COO. In fact, he's one of two high-level executives who left their companies when they saw our work in the field: Suresh Gurumani, former head of consumer banking at Barclays, which is one of our lenders, came to join us after he visited the field and saw the power of our work. He's now CEO, a position he took in late 2008 when I transitioned to chairperson at the end of SKS's first decade.

The power of our brand has drawn many companies seeking to leverage it. Wipro, Airtel, Nokia, Bajaj Allianz, and others pay for advertising space in our member passbooks, while Cavincare, a consumer packaged-goods company, pays us for providing free product samples and coupons to our members. Other companies are attracted by the wealth of data we capture about our members, which includes everything from demographic information to household assets. For example, we've launched a housing loan product with one of India's biggest banks, HDFC, which was delighted by the fact that we have detailed housing data for all our members—everything from the current size of their house to the roof quality to the wall material. This makes it easy to target housing loans with great precision.

In the last few years, though we've been approached by innumerable companies wanting to partner with us and expand into rural India, we've been very careful about making sure the products we offer are appropriate for the poor—not just cell phones, groceries, and insurance, but also products such as solar lights and water purifiers. The products must appeal to a large percentage of our members, and simultaneously be of low cost and very high quality. The result: our suppliers find new market segments, our members get high-quality goods for cheap, and we take a small percentage of the transactions. And everybody wins.

ABOVE AND BEYOND THE ECONOMIC benefits to having such large numbers, we're also able to offer our members social, educational, and health benefits. This is where yet another crucial promise of for-profit microfinance becomes apparent—another sphere where we're able to effect lasting, positive change in the lives of poor people.

Take, for example, education. The government-run education system in rural India is notoriously bad. A recent study by Harvard University professor Michael Kremer revealed that on any given school day, one out of every four teachers in government-run elementary schools doesn't show up to work. Further, of those who do show up, only half are actually teaching at any given moment.

Until now, the poor have had little choice but to send their children to these schools. But in 2008 SKS's affiliate NGO launched a pilot low-cost elementary school program, in which K–3 classes are taught in English, in rural areas. SKS NGO manages and runs the schools, which offer high-quality education with an emphasis on technology. The school tuition is set well below regular private school tuition, with the monthly fee just 260 to 340 rupees (about $5 to $7), depending on the grade. The SKS NGO academies are open to all village children—not just children of our members—and SKS Microfinance provides loans to members who cannot afford the fees.

Initiatives like these can help eradicate the very mentality of being poor. With their children getting a first-class education and training for the kind of jobs once reserved for other classes and castes, people's expectations of being poor—and staying poor for generations—begin to fade. And that's the most critical step of all in eradicating poverty.

Another idea we're exploring that has social benefit as well as potential profit impact is sanitary napkins. I hadn't realized this was even a problem in rural India, but women don't have the necessary access to sanitary products—a fact I discovered in a rather odd way. As I walked around villages, I'd often see piles of cow manure with pieces of cloth in them. I asked what they were for, and one of my field staff explained that poor women used the cloths instead of disposable sanitary napkins. After several uses, they'd throw them away in the manure pile.

The problem is, when cloth used for this purpose isn't washed properly, it can lead to health problems. This situation was made worse by the fact that rural India was increasingly seeing factory-made synthetic cloth instead of the traditional handwoven cotton cloth. The latter allows air in, making it more hygienic when used as a sanitary napkin. But the synthetics don't allow air, which leads to even more potential for infection.

I realized that if SKS could introduce access to low-cost sanitary napkins, we could potentially stem a serious health problem. In addition, we would simultaneously create and capture a brand-new market among a brand-new customer segment. Everybody wins.

We also undertake initiatives that don't generate any profits at all. These are social initiatives for which we're uniquely positioned, thanks to our distribution channels, to provide a social good. Our deworming program is a perfect example.

Worm-borne diseases affect millions of poor Indians, particularly children, every year. When these parasites enter a person's body through contact with contaminated soil or water, the results are horrific: diarrhea, stomach cramps, lethargy, vomiting, and even internal bleeding. Yet for all the agony this disease can cause, it is relatively simple to prevent—a single tablet can protect a person from the parasite's effects.

UNICEF has donated these tablets, but they sit unused in rural health care centers. The Indian government isn't distributing them, in part because of government inefficiencies, and in part because there's great mistrust among Indians for any government health initiatives involving children, so villagers probably wouldn't accept them anyway.

But even if the rural poor don't trust the government, they have grown to trust SKS. So we volunteered to have our loan officers take time from doing regular business at their meetings to help distribute these tablets. Under a pilot program we launched in 2010 to deworm children, our loan officers carried these tablets into the field, explaining to borrowers why they should take them, and answering any and all questions. In this way, we're doing our part in the global initiative to "Deworm the World," a program launched by the World Economic Forum's Young Global Leaders network, of which I'm a part.

Likewise, when there are floods or cyclones, we suspend our loan repayments and mobilize for disaster relief. During the 2008 Bihar flood, one of the worst floods in India's history, our loan officers delivered blankets and food to affected communities. We've even been included in the country's national disaster management planning discussions.

Another example of using our microfinance channel for social initiatives is our Ultra Poor Program. For-profit microfinance isn't a realistic option for the absolute poorest Indians—those who live on the equivalent of less than 50 cents US a day. These are the people who struggle simply to survive on a day-to-day basis, who spend their lives in a constant battle against chronic hunger, persistent disease, and illiteracy. Their ranks often include widows, the elderly, the disabled, and other marginalized groups who are so far out of the mainstream, and have so many basic unfulfilled needs, that they lack the stability to start businesses and meet regular payment schedules.

So SKS's nonprofit affiliate started an Ultra Poor Program—a three-pronged program that aims to bring the ultrapoor up to minimal standards of health and economic and social stability. For economic stability, the program offers members a free "asset basket" of their choice— anything from a buffalo to chickens to sheep, or nonfarm assets such as a pay telephone plus food goods to sell, or the necessities for a small teashop.

The recipients have no obligation to pay us anything in return, as the asset baskets are intended to help lift them to the next economic rung. We also assist the ultrapoor in accessing government entitlements, such as food for work programs. For health, the program offers monthly visits from a medical assistant, information sessions, and screening. And for social development, we offer group meetings, where the normally isolated ultrapoor can meet together to discuss problems and issues, and spend time building relationships.

In addition to these social initiatives, the strength of our numbers also provides political influence—an area where our members, most of whom are from backward and scheduled castes, have never had much power. When we lobby government central bank policy makers on banking reform, for example, we can inform them we represent more than 8 million members, and the number is growing. Assuming there are five people per household, that's about 40 million people—a number that makes them sit up and take notice, giving us an instant voice.

Our numbers have caught the attention of leading politicians. The Congress Party—the party of Jawaharlal Nehru and Indira Gandhi—invited my input on their election manifesto before the 2009 elections, asking what policies would best help the rural poor. Likewise, in 2008, the then–Bharatia Janata Party (BJP) chief minister of the state of Rajasthan, Vasundara Raje, as well as the BJP deputy chief minister of Bihar, Sushil Modi, both reached out to us, asking us to expand our work in their states and offering their full support. These politicians know that, with so many members across the country, our numbers could even sway elections—though we'd never purposefully do so. But numbers do matter, and they give our members clout.

Finally, SKS membership brings everyday forms of political empowerment. For one thing, we lend to women, giving them additional bargaining strength in the home. We hold our meetings in public places—a first for many scheduled caste members, who for generations weren't allowed to gather in public spaces. And in local elections, SKS members have even run for office and won, due in part to the leadership roles they've learned through their association with us.

Reaching Google territory has given our members all these benefits, and more. And we never could have gotten there if not for our aggressively for-profit system. SKS represents the best of both the nonprofit and the for-profit worlds: it's the ultimate expression of "doing well by doing good."

The financial world agreed, even in the midst of the biggest economic meltdown since the Great Depression. In October of 2008, as Lehman Brothers collapsed and the U.S. stock market plunged, we announced our latest round of investment: a stunning $75 million from Sandstone Capital, Kismet Capital, and SVB India Capital Partners—the largest investment in microfinance to date.

Our next step is to expand to other countries. We have been approached by MFIs and governments from a diverse list of countries: Sri Lanka, Nepal, China, Vietnam, Mali, Nigeria, Morocco, Egypt, Afghanistan, Peru, Colombia, and even the United States.

But as far as we have come, this is only the beginning. Microfinance is a thriving, world-changing business, and we don't intend to stop growing until every poor person in the world has access to it.

AT THE END OF A RUTTED DIRT road, about a two-hour drive northwest of Hyderabad, lies the village of Pagidiguumal. Like so many Indian villages, its unpaved streets are lined with thatched-roof huts, scrub brush, and ditches trickling with brackish water. Animals of all kinds roam among the houses—goats, chickens, stray dogs with protruding ribcages, the occasional water buffalo.

Children wander about, swinging sticks and kicking balls. Women in brightly colored saris walk toward nearby cotton fields, food and drink wrapped in bundles and balanced on their heads, ready for a day of work. Men, too, are beginning their work days, building, repairing, lifting, moving—anything that will bring in a few rupees. As the sun rises lazily in the sky, the village wakes to another day of activity.

By the side of the main road that snakes through the village, Yellamma opens her store for the day. A small mud-brick structure with whitewashed walls, the store is little bigger than a kiosk, about eight feet by ten feet, with a door cut in the front and no windows. A corrugated sheet of tin, propped up by five knotty pieces of lumber, acts as an awning, and a green plastic payphone is attached to the outside wall. Yellamma hangs out a few dozen bags of crunchy corn snacks, indicating she's open for business.

Inside, the store offers a whole range of goods: individual foil packets of shampoo, laundry soap, and pain reliever; sodas; snacks and toothbrushes; even grains and lentils. Before stores like Yellamma's opened, the people of villages like Pagidiguumal had few stores to choose from. They had to accept the prices charged by the main—typically upper-class—store owners or walk to the next village, or take the bus, or pay for a ride, to buy these most basic goods. Now, they can simply walk down the street.

Yellamma opened her store with a 4,000-rupee loan, about $80, from SKS, which enabled her to buy her first batch of goods. By your standards and mine, the profit she makes on her store is minuscule, perhaps a few dollars a week. But for Yellamma, these tiny sums, earned week after week, add up to more than she needs.

And this store isn't Yellamma's only venture. With another, earlier loan from SKS, she purchased four water buffalo, which she keeps tied up in a makeshift manger next to her house. The buffalo give milk, some of which she uses for her family and some of which she sells. And because the buffalo cost virtually nothing to maintain, the money she made from them immediately went to paying her loan installment. Now that her first loan is completely paid off, Yellamma has an asset that costs her nothing, but will provide for her for years to come.

From her thin green sari, to her modest jewelry, to the absence of a bindi dot on her forehead, I can tell that Yellamma is a Dalit, or untouchable. The fact that she was able to open her own store is an acknowledgment that she's a valued member of society, a person who is fulfilling an important need for her village. The store gives her a way to rise above her status, which used to be an impossibility for a woman in her position.

Yellamma walks me to her house, just a few steps away. It looks almost exactly like the store, only bigger, with the same whitewashed walls and corrugated tin awning. In the front, to the left of the door, a brick fire pit spews gray smoke skyward as a pot of water sits boiling. She invites me in, and I take off my sandals before stepping through the door.

When my eyes adjust to the dim light inside, I see that the house consists of nothing more than one rectangular room, with thin bedding and a blanket rolled up in one corner. But then I look to the other end of the room. And there I see a television.

"It's color!" she says, following my gaze. A color TV? I have to laugh.

"Where did you get it?" I ask.

"My son bought it for me," she says. "He works for SKS."

When I had met Yellamma earlier in the day, I had no idea her son worked for us. With more than two thousand branches across India and our blistering pace of growth, we're long past the time when I could get to know—or even meet—all our twenty-three thousand of employees.

Yet I wasn't surprised that Yellamma's son worked for us. Especially given the pace of our growth, we've always sought out new employees who are sons and daughters of our members, who come from the same impoverished communities as the borrowers they serve. To avoid a conflict of interest, her son would of course never work in a region where he had anything to do with his mother's loan or her loan group. But I was happy to hear that SKS had helped not only Yellamma, but the next generation of her family, escape the poverty that the luck of the draw had bestowed on them.

I thought back to the woman in the faded purple sari, all those years ago—the woman who asked the question that changed my life: "Am I not poor, too?" And I couldn't help but contrast her with smiling Yellamma, proudly telling me about how SKS has helped her family.

"Am I not doing well?" she asked. Yes, she was.

ACKNOWLEDGMENTS

There are many people who have helped achieve what has been captured in this book.

First and foremost are SKS members. They are extraordinary women—poor women—who struggle against myriad challenges to make better lives for themselves and their families. These women are confident, entrepreneurial, and downright tough. Their sheer strength of spirit is astounding. I am constantly inspired by what they have been able to accomplish. I have learned a lot from them and continue to do so.

Second is my family. I know that I follow in the footsteps of my paternal grandmother, Akula Ranganayakamma, and my paternal grandfather, Akula Venkatramiah. My maternal grandmother, Dhaduvai Shakunthala, gently guided me during my post college years in India. Though my maternal grandfather, Dhaduvai Kishtaiah, passed away when I was young, it is wonderful to know that I probably have walked along many of the same Telangana village roads that he once did. There is, of course, my large, boisterous, immigrant extended clan, spread across the United States. Through the years, we have had philosophical differences, fierce family debates, and tons of fun.

At every stage and with every turn, my family has been there. My parents, Akula Krishna and Padma Krishna, have been pillars of strength. My brother Gautham Akula and cousin Prashant Mitta are my closest confidants. I could not have survived in India without my cousin Chandana Gadwala; her parents G.V. Ramana Babu and G.V. Kalpana have guided me in the early SKS days. I have also had financial support from—and home offices in—each of my paternal uncles' homes in India—that of A.V. Panduranga Rao and A. Shakunthala, A.V. Hanumanth and Vijaya Laxmi Rao, and A.V. Mohan and Vidya Rao.

Each and every member of my family contributed money to help get SKS started. The most notable is the generous support and vote of confidence from Ravi and Pratibha Reddy and their partners Sandeep and Vidhya Tungare. Without their support, none of my early SKS work would have been possible. I am also indebted to Jagdish and Shanta Chandra, Srinivas and Swatantra Mitta, Satyamurthy and Sashikala Abkari, Ashok and Swarup Pilly, Ameresh and Swarnakala Kura, the late Chandrashekhar Thunga and Vijaya Thunga, Govind and Jyothi Rao, and Kumuda and Janardhan Reddy. Others, such as Suma Reddy, gave me the invaluable gifts of their time and their tremendous effort. Meanwhile, many friends have also contributed generously, including Sanjiv Sidhu, Lekha Singh, Srikanth Ravi, Sudhakar Ravi, and the wonderful people at the India Development Service, especially Anita Deshmukh, Nila Vora, and Jagjit Jain.

I am also indebted to my mentor Biksham Gujja and many friends from the Deccan Development Society, including K. Narsanna, K. Padma, V. Gurumurthy, Uma Maheshwari, and all my friends in Pastapur and Shamshudinpur.

If I started to thank everyone at SKS, the list would go on for pages. But I must mention some people.

No one in the SKS family played a more influential role in my life than the late V. Sitaram Rao who shepherded me and who stepped in to lead SKS when we needed him most. Sitaram, I think of you always and miss you dearly.

I am also grateful to Vithal Rajan, founding chair of SKS NGO; Gurcharan Das, chair emeritus of SKS NBFC; our COO, M.R. Rao, who is like a brother to me and whose friendship I cherish; our CFO, S. Dilliraj, who has been rock solid and whose quiet perseverance is inspiring; our CEO, Suresh Gurumani, who has helped SKS take a big leap. Then there's the field team of the early days: S.Rama Laxmi, K. Nirmala, the stalwart T. Sandhya Rani, M. Rangamma, B. Basavaraj, K. Sailu, K. Pradeep Kumar, J. Srinivas, the late M. Sanjeev, M. Sangiah, N. Nageswar,

K. Hemanth Kumar, K. Manikyam, S. Ramulu, B. Moguliah, P. Savithri, J. Venkat Reddy, M. Ravinder, Ch. Balaiah, S. Mallesham, M. Siddiah, J. Narsimulu, S. Vinod Rao, V. Ravinder, M. Yadaiah, T. Mallesh, J.S. Chalam, M. Pandurangam, G. Bhaskar, G. Sampath, B. Rajaiah, Md. Raheem Pasha, M. Jaganathan, B. Veeresham, B. Bichappa, Ch. Venkat Reddy, K. Sadanandam, K. Yadagiri, K.R. Nagaraju, S, Shankuntala, P. Jayamma, M. Shiva Kumar, P. Laxman Yadav. B.Tirupathaiah, S. Saritha, and M. Ramesh.

Our early head office team also played an instrumental role, including K. Veera Reddy, Kanchan Pandhre, Ashish Damani, P.V. Kalyanachakrawarthy, Ch. Nagaraju, T. Shashi Kumar, K. Sridhar, D. Rama, S.V.S. Durga Prasad. On a personal level, I am grateful to Manish Kumar, P. Srinivas, K. Vijaya Reddy, Saheba Sahni, Kathy Skoby, Amy Yee, and Sivani Shankar.

Along the way, many others helped take us to higher levels, including Kavitha Kuruganti, the late Shyam Mohan, Bala Krishnamurthy, Praseeda Kunam, the late M. Basavaraj, Jennifer Meehan, Gautam Ivatury, Anu Pillai Mitta, Jennifer Leonard, Chris Turillo, and Paul Breloff.

To members of our core management team—K.V. Rao, Lakshminarayan Subramanyam, V. Ramesh, Pradeep Kalra, Atul Takle, Sunil Bansal, Kanchan Pandhre, Ashish Damani, P. Balaji, Sandeep Ralhan, Vinod Kumar,

Manish Kumar, Ashish Pipaliya, GSV Ramu, Monica Verma, P. Seshagiri, A. Srikanth, Harish Singh, Joachim Sequeira, Chitra Sharan, Amy Yee, as well as Kiran Kumar, Rashmi Singh, Gopi Krishna, Ruchi Singh, Vinod Joshi, and Animesh Anand—thank you for believing in our mission.

None of this could have happened without our funders, especially Vinod Khosla who made a pioneering investment in SKS and who has provided invaluable support to the SKS Trusts. Other major early funders include the Echoing Green Foundation led by Cheryl Dorsey; Friends of Women's World Banking led by Vijaya Lakshmi Das; Grameen Foundation USA led by Alex Counts; Unitus and its affiliates led by Mike Murray, Geoff Davis, and Chris Brookfield; Brij Mohan; R.M. Malla and the great team at the Small Industries Development Bank of India; Sequoia led by Sumir Chadha; Kismet Capital led by Ashish Lakhanpal; Sandstone led by Paresh Patel; Yatish Trading; Bikky Khosla; Silicon Valley Bank led by Ash Lilani in India; the Bill and Melinda Gates Foundation; the Schwab Foundation; and the Khemka Foundation. Meanwhile, Phil Smith and George Kaiser gave critical support to the SKS Trusts.

In the broader microfinance world, I continue to learn from Professor Muhammad Yunus of the Grameen Bank, Ela Bhatt of SEWA, Vijay Mahajan of BASIX, David Gibbons of Cashpor, Nachiket Mor of IFMR, and Maria

Otero, former CEO of ACCION. You are wonderful role models.

A special thanks to Marc Kadish, David Carpenter, and Ashish Prasad of Mayer Brown LLP, the law firm that provided SKS invaluable pro-bono assistance as we converted from a nonprofit to a for-profit.

Finally, I am grateful to Lisa Dickey for all her help and guidance. I also owe a debt of gratitude to Howard Yoon and Gail Ross for helping me get this book published; Kirsten Sandberg for believing in me; and the wonderful team at Harvard Business Press, led by Jacque Murphy and Ania Wieckowski.

A Note on the Stories and Quoted Material

The stories and quotations in this book have been reconstructed as faithfully as possible from memory: things that were either said directly to me or recounted to me by another source. Any errors contained in these retellings are my own.

ABOUT THE AUTHOR

VIKRAM AKULA is the Founder and Chairperson of SKS Microfinance, one of the leading microfinance institutions in the world. With more than twenty years experience in development, he is a sought-after public speaker, and in 2006, *Time* magazine named him one of the world's 100 most influential people. A former community organizer with the Deccan Development Society in India, Akula holds a BA from Tufts, an MA from Yale, a PhD from the University of Chicago, and was a Fulbright Scholar. He also worked as a management consultant with McKinsey & Company and has received several awards, including being named a World Economic Forum Young Global Leader (2008), Schwab Social Entrepreneur of the Year in India (2006), the Ernst & Young Start-Up Entrepreneur of the Year in India (2006), and an Echoing Green Fellow (1998–2002). He has been profiled in media ranging from CNN to the front page of the *Wall Street Journal*. For more information, see SKS's Web site, www.sksindia.com.